You Can Too

How an Aflac Rookie
Built the Business in a Year

JONNY BURGESS

iUniverse, Inc.
Bloomington

You Can Too

How an Aflac Rookie Built the Business in a Year

iUniverse books may be ordered through booksellers or by contacting:

iUniverse
1663 Liberty Drive
Bloomington, IN 47403
www.iuniverse.com
1-800-Authors (1-800-288-4677)

ISBN: 978-1-4620-3969-2 (sc)
ISBN: 978-1-4620-3971-5 (hc)
ISBN: 978-1-4620-3970-8 (e)

Printed in the United States of America

iUniverse rev. date: 10/4/2011

Foreword

AFLAC REGIONAL SALES COORDINATOR MAINE/NEW HAMPSHIRE

Let me prepare you that the book you are about to read will change the picture you may have about how to effectively sell Aflac. If anyone tells you that selling Aflac is easy, it is simply not true. It is true however that Aflac is simple to explain assuming of course that you have someone to explain it to. The actual appointment setting process is relatively difficult for anyone who insists on doing it the hard way. Knocking on door after door expecting the business owner to not only welcome you, but fall down at your feet being thankful that you have finally honored him with your presence is a fantasy. Without question, cold calling can be extremely difficult and nerve racking. The lack of effective cold calling has chased away more new Aflac agents from the business than all other possible reasons combined. If the most difficult and frustrating part of the Aflac sale for you is actually setting the appointment with the business owner than I bring you extraordinarily good news! Jonny Burgess, the number one Aflac account opener in the country in 2009, his very first year as an Associate, has turned the difficult "cold call", the part of the sale perceived as absolute drudgery, into a rather pleasant experience which can yield not only 8-10 appointments a day, but quickly open the mind of the business owner to immediately sign the

M-0138 at your very first meeting. After reading "You Can Too!" and applying its techniques, you will never again have to feel or be perceived as a professional visitor trying to get an appointment or calling on the same account over and over hoping for a signed M-0138.

The mid-term election of 2010 will soon begin to change the way the American employer looks at National Health Care. This book "You Can Too" will rightly position you for the upcoming media discussion which will focus on the costs and gaps of Health Care with more of the focus pointing to the obvious need for Supplemental Insurance. Whether you are a seasoned Aflac veteran or a new struggling Associate still trying to determine whether or not Aflac is the right career for you, I highly encourage you to devour each and every page of this "How To" book by Jonny Burgess with your mind wide open, excited about being positioned with the right company having the right solutions at the exact right time in history.

Looking forward to your success,

Bill Henry

Contents

INTRODUCTION

Y ou may be wondering, "Am I in the right place?" You may be a veteran of Aflac and be wondering if there is some magic formula that can propel you to success. You might even be a coordinator wondering if there is a simplified 'fast-track' that will get your agents out of mediocrity and into excellence. The answer to all of these questions is, "Yes!"

Just a year and a half ago, I was at a very similar cross-roads in my life. 'Literally' bankrupt, my 10 year food business that had succumbed to the economic climate had gone under. I was desperately trying to provide for my 5 children as a single father, win the heart (and belief) of my new fiancé, and not allow the circumstances around me determine my destiny or rob me of my dreams, which can be a tall feat when you are in survival mode.

I had been half-heartedly studying to pass the insurance license exam, thinking selling insurance on the side could be a viable second income as I pushed through a terrible climate in food sales, my prior sales position. Just 3 years earlier, times had been good. I was a sales manager for a national food service company, managing on average a dozen sales reps. I thought things were secure and my income seemed comfortable, (though now looking back, I will never work the 70 hours-a-week I was then). During my Aflac sales-school, I was sneaking extra snack packages of granola for later because that is all I would have to eat, I was that broke!

Fast forward to today…Life is good! I am living in a beautiful dream home with the in-ground pool and Jacuzzi on 4 acres. I take 6 full week-long vacations a year. I enjoy a comfortable 6-figure income, and already reap the fruits of my labor receiving thousands of dollars a month in residuals and renewals. Most importantly, I am able to spend countless long weekends, and virtually every evening at home with my beautiful wife and children. I have my life back!

I am extremely driven and competitive, but even more than that-I love to teach. From teaching children's church, to teaching mixed martial arts, to taking sales reps in the field, I have a real passion to teach others, motivate them, and help them experience greatness, even to a level they never thought possible.

In this book you are now holding in your hand, I will challenge you to think and dream bigger than you have ever dared, get you to realize that you definitely CAN do this, and then show you a very simple, duplicatable system and plan of action that will work for you if you simply work the plan, stay the course, and discipline yourself to do the daily requirements it takes to succeed in this business.

Best of all, you will make money NOW. And most importantly, it will not be at the expense of your family. I want everyone reading (and applying) this system to increase in every area of their life, not just financially. In the next two months you will experience a steady stream of cash flow, set into motion an enormous wealth-building enterprise, and experience an unbelievable lifestyle within the next two years!

I believe that you are not reading this book by accident. 'Your' time is now, and your future awaits! Lets get started.

WHY AFLAC?

There are certainly countless opportunities out there, so why would Aflac be the right one for you (or anybody)?

What are the three highest paid professions in the United States?

1. Doctors

2. Attorneys

3. Commission sales reps (note that salary plus commission ranks #22)

If building the life of your dreams drives you, then what options are available to you to pursue the American Dream? You could very well pursue either of the first two listed above. However, is that medical doctor extremely wealthy and fulfilled the moment he receives his diploma from med school? No, in fact he most likely has already invested 7 to 11 years of his/her life, and now realizes serious debt obligations thanks to sizeable school loans that are now due. Furthermore, he now has to 'seek' employment (like everybody else) unless he determines to have his or her own practice. In which case he now has to seek further funding to lease an office, pay for advertising, take out more loans for his dentist chair and drill system or whatever else is necessary (not to mention malpractice insurance). Then he has to interview and hire several operators, nurses, assistants etc, that by the way want to be paid 'next-week' because they are just looking for a week to week paycheck and cannot wait until you build up that client base. If they stay the course they certainly WILL be successful, but it is certainly no get-rich-quick plan to say the least. Attorneys have a similar uphill climb, to try to rise above the countless $40,000/year lawyers that work for other firms, until they someday make 'partner' or open their own practice.

I am not trying to discourage anybody that wants to be a lawyer or doctor. If that is your driving passion, then you shouldn't do anything else. But if you find yourself soul-searching for your purpose in life and your career destiny, or perhaps find yourself at a cross-roads in life 20 years in as I was (whether it is due to divorce, business failure, bankruptcy, sickness, or anything else) then sales is literally a phenomenal option. Furthermore, contrary to options #1 and 2 above, in sales you can experience the 6 figure incomes within the first 5 years (I've done it in my second). And from there the sky is the limit. A quick look on the leader report on RPM, and it is evident that many even have 7 figure incomes. That's a lot of zeros!

Then again, there are also a lot of things that you can sell. You could sell cars, houses, copiers, medical devices, food, cosmetics etc. The difference between insurance sales and all of these however, is the residual income. I coined the phrase that I am 'ambitiously lazy!' I love the fact that work I am doing today will pay me for years to come. In just 18 short months I already make well over $1000/week before I even get out of bed! I have huge goals, and some include significant amounts of time traveling around this great country and across the globe. My personal goal is to get my monthly residuals to the point where they exceed $50,000/month. I decided that over a year ago, and then put together a plan, and I am actually just ahead of schedule.

Then again, there are also other insurance companies out there, but having been in the front lines for the past year and a half, I can very comfortably say that I am working for the best insurance company in the world. And if you haven't yet comprehended the incredible recognition of 'the Duck' you need to give that serious consideration. Why would anybody want to work for anybody but the best? On top of that, as you get to know the dynamics and mission of the company at heart, you will know that you are on the right team.

If you need to take some time to meditate, contemplate, or pray about whether this opportunity is for you, then take the time, soul-search and decide. But if you have already decided, then don't look back, lets roll up our sleeves, and take action.

Whereas I do believe in 'sharpening the axe before you cut the tree', I also very much believe that most of the sharpening takes place as you are swinging away. So please, don't try to get it perfect, just learn the basic fundamentals to this system, and then go out and have them make you money.

THE SECRET TO SUCCESS

L et me ask you a question. What do you think would happen if we dropped Donald Trump in an unknown city, and stripped him of all his money, favor, advantages and connections? Now fast-forward ten years, is there any doubt in your mind that he would be a millionaire? (Personally I think that it would take him less than 3). Why is that? Simply, he would undoubtedly 'believe' he could, and so he would.

So why does anybody else doubt the same results from themselves? It is the power of believing. I believe this with every fiber of my being. If you knew you couldn't fail, what would you aim for? Honestly, ask yourself that. What incredible lofty goal would you strive for if, in your mind, success was certain?

Think about that teenage boy in high school. Asking the prettiest girl in school out on a date would be a whole lot easier if he was sure that she would say yes. So comes the element called 'fear of failure'. But what the great success stories of recent past tell us is that any failure we experience is simply a temporary set-back, and it is feed-back that will actually tell you how to get it closer the next time.

If you don't understand the power of the mind, then you are not going to begin to tap into the greatness that you possess. The problem is that we have tried in the past, failure or rejection didn't feel very good, and so we gave up. If that is you then shame on you, especially if you are a parent, because you have an obligation to demonstrate that it is okay to get knocked down, but it is pathetic if you stay down!

It is a well-known fact that 4 out of 5 businesses fail within the first 5 years. Believe me, think about starting a business and share your inspiration with your 'friends', and they will quote this most accurate statistic and warn you to rethink your great idea. But what they don't tell you (because they are clueless) is that when someone fails as a business owner, but then gives it another attempt, the second time around they are almost 80% assured of success! That is because they learned from their experience, and refused to stay down! So if your fear of failure is from a past unsuccessful endeavor, then look at that as an advantage and as an asset. If you haven't yet had the opportunity to fail, but are wise enough and mature enough to learn from the experiences of others, then you can actually save yourself some hard knocks. Experience is indeed the best teacher, but it just may be somebody else's experience that you can benefit from.

But, DON'T BE A BABY ELEPHANT! I marvel at the massive size and power of the elephants whenever I am at the zoo or circus. What I learned however, is that when that elephant is just a baby, its trainer puts a metal band around his leg, connected to a rope, and the other end is tied to a stake that is pounded into the ground. That baby animal tugs and tugs and tugs on that rope trying to free itself from the metal band, but after countless attempts and aimless struggles, that baby finally gives up tugging on that rope. "What's the point" it thinks, "I cant get free". Years later however, when we see that baby animal which has since grown into an enormous beast, there is still that metal band that keeps it within a rope's length. Even though that 8000 pound giant could 'easily' take out that stake with a simple tug, and take a large part of the earth with it, it won't even try-because he gave up trying years earlier. Don't you be that baby elephant, don't give up trying to be or accomplish something great. Break the ropes that hold you back, there are only in your mind.

If you are skeptical about the power of the mind, let me tell you about Nick Sitzman. Nick, a 30-year-old married father of 2, had jumped a railroad car to get an easy transport to the next town. As circumstance would have it, the train retired operations until the following day, and Nick found himself locked in a freezer box-car. His relentless pounding from inside the boxcar and cries for help were to no avail. There came a point where he gave up as his body temperature dropped. He actually carved into the wood from inside the car a message to his children, but also the trembling etch of "I AM SO COLD". They found Nick Sitzman dead the next day in that freezer car. The kicker-the freezer unit wasn't even on! Yet because the power of believing is so powerful, the autopsy revealed that Nick had in fact died of hypothermia, because he 'believed' he was freezing to death!

I contemplated awhile when I first heard that story years ago. Not only how powerful the mind is, but trying to figure how I could harness that same power.

Even more amazing is the story of Viet-Nam POW tortures. Gagged soldiers would be forced to watch as a fellow GI would be blindfolded and strapped down on a table with his arms stretched out to both sides. The blindfolded GI was shown 2 metal buckets and a knife prior to the tie-down. The torturing Viet-Kong would then take the knife and slice open both wrists, and the soldier would hear the agonizing sound of hearing his own blood drip from both wrists into the bucket. They usually bled to death within 15 minutes. But then the same sequence would play out except this time they would drag a sharp piece of ice across the wrists of the next blindfolded GI, not really even cutting him. Then the ice was set on the end of the table, so that as it melted, the familiar dripping into the bucket sound was heard again (only this time it was only melting water). That soldier would die in about 25 minutes. Thinking he was bleeding to death, the brain eventually told the heart to stop beating.

This same amazing power can also be tapped into doing great and amazing things. The power of visualization is awesome. I remember the first time I wrote down that, "I would like to write 80 policies at today's enrollment", and then pictured sitting with dozens and dozens of people at the laptop who were lining up to get Aflac from me...Well that enrollment took more than just that day, but by the end of it I had in fact written 70+ policies, and along with some other activity that week, cleared over $8000 that week in advances just a few months into the business.

Since then, I have taken images from the 'my statements' link on the web site under 'direct deposits', printed out the copies of 'checks', and then added zeros to the total and simply whited out the decimal and replaced it with a comma. Thus I have a 'check' for $12,000 that I stare at daily, which represents one of my goals: to receive a month-end residual check exceeding $12,000 by the end of 2010. I started doing this before I even had a positive monthly balance, but today (just 18 months into the business) I am already receiving monthly statements for over half that amount. (And you can too!) I have another one for $50,000, representing my 5 year monthly income goal. I strongly urge you to do something similar, even if it feels silly or awkward at first. The 'belief' will come. (By the way, the person who gave me this idea did a similar thing years ago when he was flat broke, and now makes hundreds of millions a year!). Don't even let that number intimidate you. Why not you? As you visualize that monthly sum of money (whatever that number is for you) picture how you would spend that money. Remember, this will be your monthly income, not a random windfall of money. Do you give significant support to your favorite ministry or charity? Would you make extra payments on your mortgage (triple mortgage payments pay off a 30 year mortgage in just under 7!). Would you be traveling much more regularly, and to where? What are you wearing and what do you drive? By the way, I close my eyes and make sure I won't get interrupted as I visualize so that I don't get distracted. Another great place for this exercise is a hot bath.

I am about to go into my fast-track success system, but without the element of belief, it will be to no avail. Don't just go through the motions, but rather create a burning desire to build this thing, and build it big. Dare to dream bigger than you have ever dared to dream.

THE GAME PLAN

The first step was actually determining your 'Why' followed by the belief that your efforts will be rewarded by tremendous success. Now, lets actually hit the trenches.

The absolute key to fast success is stuffing the pipeline with constant activity, and targeting the smaller businesses to produce immediate cash flow.

Of course the larger accounts are fun and super profitable, but consider this advice, "you aren't ready for those yet". Furthermore, lets assume that you need immediate cash flow. The system I am about to lay out will net you hundreds of dollars 'next week', and will insure a steady stream of income, and be creating wealth at the same time. Also, keep in mind that by closing these small businesses at rapid fire pace, you are going to hone your skills and instill such confidence in yourself, that when the slightly larger accounts come to you, you will be ready! Believe me, you don't want to blow it when the opportunity to close that mammoth account comes your way.

Most important is the immediate stream of income. How are we going to insure that? Simply put, the activity schedule of Book ten/Run ten. I am going to lead you every step of the way, don't worry. We will dissect every stage of the game. But for now, assume that this system of activity will work for you. Don't worry about being perfect at this yet.

Like any sales, this is in fact a numbers game, however, I believe that with this system, you can 'cheat' the numbers. You can literally double both your income AND your time-off 'this year'.

Again, I am going to assume that you need cash 'this month' not simply down the road. If this was just a turtle-paced accumulation of residual income, then I would not be here! I had to pay my mortgage every month, not explain to the mortgage company that I will be making boo-koo bucks a year from now. I needed to make money immediately. If you are fortunate enough that you are in the position that you can coast because you have a steady stream of income anyway, then that can be an asset yet it can also cripple your sense of urgency. If that is you, what will propel you to activity is daring to take your income and lifestyle to the next level, regardless of where you are at.

For now, lets assume that you have acquired the skills that are going to be spelled out in the following chapters. Lets assume that your activity is honest and your results are average. Here we go:

BOOK TWO / RUN TWO

My first mentor in this business did me a tremendous favor. He broke down my mid-range income goals into daily activity. Simply put, I asked him what I would have to do to immediately make $5000/ month, and within a year be making six figures. He told me that if I was to book 2 appointments a day, and run 2 appointments a day, that formula would bring me the results I was after. The good news is that I was naïve enough to believe him. The sad news is that he didn't model that for me and I don't believe he is even in the business today. But he did me a tremendous favor by giving me that formula.

Lets assume that you are targeting small businesses (local garages, gift shops, and hair salons), your employer presentation is adequate, and your employee presentation is average and that you get fair results. If you are actually meeting with 10 business owners (decision makers) a week, and just 4 of them have you come in to talk with their employees, and you employ the '3 accidents and out' mentality, you will net about $1200/week. Lets see how:

The average commission advance on 3 accident policies is about $200. It could be slightly less if they are only individuals, but could also easily be more with family plans. Of course there might be 5 or 6 mechanics instead of 3, and you very well may up-sell other products at the laptop. But for now, lets assume the '3 accidents and out' mindset.

I (with the 'secret' opening line I will share with you in the next chapter) pop in unannounced to that shopkeeper on a Monday morning. I ask for 5 minutes when I am back in town on Wednesday afternoon. On Wednesday afternoon I wow him with my 5-minute accident presentation (which I will also show you), and he has me come in on Friday morning to speak with his mechanics. Lets say 3 of the 4 employees each get an accident policy. I then drive to the nearest McDonalds with WIFI, transmit the business, and Bingo, $200 for me, direct deposited in about 48 hours. Turnaround time-approximately 10 days from opening line to payday! It is literally that simple (not necessarily easy-but simple). Now you "rinse, lather, repeat". You do it again and again and again.

Back to our average results of only 4 in 10 employers saying yes to your presentation. At the bare minimum, you have made $800 this week! And there are always a few businesses that surprise you with their 8 employees, not 3. Furthermore, an up-sell at the laptop of a dental, cancer, or life policy-even occasionally, will put you over the top and net you over $5000... this month!

THIS SHOULD NOT BE AN EVERY DAY ALL DAY COLD-CALLING JOB!!

I started as my mentor had suggested, booking 2 appointments a day, and then running 2 a day. But very early on I realized (again being 'ambitiously lazy') that I could just book my 10 appointments in one afternoon (and you will be able to too after you learn the art of the 'secret' opening line), and the rest of the time I am wowing small business owners and enrolling their employees.

If you are skeptical as to whether or not this can really be done... don't be. I more or less invented this mindset of close 3 accidents and out... "Next!" out of necessity. You see my first business owner that signed the m-0138 was a small donut shop. They definitely bought into the concept, but the presentation got rescheduled four times because of ice storms and power outages here in New Hampshire. Unfortunately that same mentor had told me to keep my schedule clear so as to really service this small chain of donut shops, and that I would make a ton of money. "Yee-haw" I thought...until it got rescheduled 4 times!! I did eventually write about 15 accident policies and made well over $1000, but I 'starved' in the meantime. I am now kind of glad that that happened though, because very early on I told myself that I would never again have all my hopes on one account. I determined right then and there to always continually stuff the pipeline with so much activity that I would never again miss a steady flow of income.

That was all in the month of December 2008. During the month of January, I was working on my business owner presentation, selling a couple of direct policies, but most importantly, coming up with this 'system'. (Oh yeah, I was also planning for my upcoming wedding in February)

In the first week of February 2009, I closed 4 groups!

I got married on February 20th, and went on a Caribbean cruise for my honeymoon, but when I came back I was able to pick up right where I left off-and I closed 21 groups by the end of March!

I ended my rookie year as the #1 account opener in the entire country, before I was promoted to DSC in week 52.

Listen, I can play harder than anybody I know. But I became obsessed with a work hard/play hard mindset that consumed me! I was able to streamline the system to the point that I even took Fridays off all year, and took another 5 weeks off for vacation with my wife and children by the end of last year, besides countless long weekends camping. But when I was working, I was working. I didn't waste time memorizing the web site, learning the commission structures (I still have no idea how they work-I just know that I get deposits almost every single day), or doing any activity that would not generate income.

Think of it, you are in a business that has a schedule of talking to business owners during business hours, and enrolling their employees during the work-day. I came from working 70 hours a week, and tons of nights and weekends. Now I have my life back!

I hope you realize what you have in this opportunity. Chances are that if you have been previously self-employed that you may be able to appreciate what I am talking about. I have friends for example in the restaurant business that start at 5:00am, never get a day off, have to deal with constant inventory and employee issues, and are totally stressed all the time! (I just have to remember to order brochures and ducks!) And I am making more than them, and can also have the time to enjoy it. I 'desperately' want to pass on to you what I have learned and figured out.

I expect these same results for everybody on my team, and it works for my associates as well as for me. The northeast territory is comprised of over 10,000 associates from 12 states, and usually our 'new little district' has at least 3 agents in the top 10!

And guess what…"You Can Too!"

THE OPENING LINE

In my opinion, the #1 essential skill that you have to master is the opening line. There is a science to what I am about to teach you.

Before I start, I want to mention that this may be different, in fact very different, than what you have been taught before. If what you are already doing is working great, then by all means, don't change a thing. Maybe you should proceed to the next chapter. But if you are experiencing frustrations, or think of this as a cold-calling job, then you need to take note.

With this approach, you will be able to book a week's worth of activity in half a day. The rest of the time will be occupied running appointments and enrolling employees...the things that make you money.

If you are a baseball enthusiast, then you've heard of Ricky Henderson. He is known as the greatest base stealer of all-time. He had such a knack; an incredible jump, lightning speed, and a remarkable read of the pitcher. He stole over 1400 bases during his career. Second base hundreds of times, third base as well, and even on occasion, home plate! However, Ricky was never able to steal first. The reason for this analogy is that no matter how well you know the Aflac products, how fast you are on SNG, or how fantastic your employee presentation is,...

unless you can book that appointment with the business owner, you'll never get the chance to demonstrate any of those.

Allow me to mention the explicit instructions given to my oldest daughter, who runs the front desk at this area's most up-scale bed and breakfast. The owner said, "Whenever a sales rep calls and asks to speak with me, let them know that I am 'unavailable', and then ask for their name and number, read it back to them so that they know you got it correctly, *and then right after you hang up, crumble up the paper and throw it in the trash!"* I NEVER use the phone. By the way, I stopped by this same B&B, gave her the opening line that I am about to give you, and days later made about $1500 at the enrollment!

The key is to have the mindset that 'you are Aflac', you are in a hurry, and in high demand, and extremely busy. I am not asking them to buy anything, meet me to buy something, over even mention much of what I do at all. I am simply 'finally' able to meet you, and apologetically explain that as much as I would like to stay and meet them further, I've really 'gotta go'. I am however going to happen to be in the area a few days from now, and could possibly come by for 5 minutes, but even then, I won't have much time for you.

HERE IT IS:

"Hi, how are you? I haven't had a chance to meet you yet. I'm Jonny the Aflac guy. I work for a lot of your neighbors. Unfortunately I am on the way to Manchester right now, but I am going to be back in town here on Friday morning. Say, if I stop by with a brochure, could you give me 5 minutes to show you how Aflac works? You've seen the duck on TV right?" (They say "sure" or "yes", and even though they may be answering the 'have you seen the duck' question, I got my yes!) I conclude with **"Great, see you on Friday, do have a card? Thanks, Have a great day."**

You may be thinking that couldn't possibly work that easily, but guess what, it does. It works time after time after time. In fact, to book my 10 appointments for the week, I usually am popping in on just over a dozen businesses. If I have to stop at 20, I definitely have my 10 appointments booked. At 3 or 4, the owner might not be in, or it may be a corporate store, and maybe 2 or 3 already have Aflac, but the others will meet with me. And think to yourself for a moment, "Why wouldn't they?"

I have now been a DSC for about 6 months, and one of my recruits, John Favre, that made fast start (as have 4 others already) thinks he figured out why this simple approach works. His theory is that by letting them off the hook today, they almost obligate themselves to 'give you 5 minutes' when you pop back in days later.

This may seem very 'loosey-goosey' to you, but it works. Our little district has already closed about 70 groups in the first half of this year.

I encourage you to repeat this line over and over again, until it becomes 'rewind-play, rewind-play'. I would also caution you not to drift from this script. A subtle change could make a very large difference. Another one of my recruits, Tim Wakeman, (also a super-fast start), had some frustrations during his first day in the field. All day of cold calling netted him only one appointment. He insisted that he was using the 'exact' line, and that it didn't work. So, I met him in the field and rehearsed it with him. It went something like, "Hi, I'm Tim your local Aflac rep, and I sell insurance to a lot of your neighbors…" It sounded the same in his head, but obviously-not quite. We fine-tuned it 'til it was exact, then sent him back out the next day. The results were, 21 calls, 4 already had Aflac, out of the rest, Tim got 12 appointments, and went on to make well over $1000 in his first week. In fact, he hadn't even been to sales school yet. The following week on the 'field day' of sales school, he booked a state-record 24 appointments in one day! By the way, this business takes heart much more than it takes skill. New Hampshire has the second hardest insurance exam in the country, and it took Tim 6 attempts before he passed! Now that is a guy who has the kind of tenacity that I can work with and teach. Now 9 months into the business, he has won 3 free trips including state convention and Triple Crown.

Think of yourself as in quicksand. If you stand there, I promise you will sink! Don't think you are helping matters by trying to incorporate all kinds of small talk. There will be time for that later. For now, remember that busy business owners are busy. They so respect and appreciate that you were just cordial, but were in and out within seconds. That way they are also more apt to believe that you only need '5 minutes' when you drop back by. You MUST think of yourself as on par with this business owner. You are also a very busy business owner, and that, he can relate to.

Occasionally a business owner may even ask for a more specific time, and that's fine if you can do it. But I purposely want to leave it loose, because remember that you are going to be running at least a half dozen of these appointments on that day. Sometimes that '5 minute' meeting turns into a home-run, and you actually conduct an employee presentation and enroll them all on that same morning. So I don't want to have to leave a slam-dunk to go see another ER because of a schedule conflict.

Believe me, this can get crazy. Twice I have actually conducted enrollments and closed 4 groups in a day! I have had to reschedule employee presentations and enrollments because I have double booked.

It is a great problem to have, but is still a little chaotic. But, I am still home almost every day when the kids are getting off the bus!

THE POWER OF A NAME

One small thing that you can do to tweak the opening line just a little, is to try and say, "Hey, you must be Joe. I haven't had a chance to meet you yet. I'm Jonny the Aflac guy. I work for a lot of your neighbors. Unfortunately, I am on the way to Manchester right now, but I am going to be back in town here on Friday morning. Say, if I stop by with a brochure, could you give me 5 minutes to show you what Aflac does? You've seen the duck on TV right?"

The only difference, I mentioned his name. But how did I know his name was Joe? I peeked out of the corner of my eye and picked it up off of his business card holder on the counter. Weird thing is, they never ask me how I knew their name. You can also look for the newspaper article that is framed on the wall. Under the picture of his grand opening or charitable donation, the caption will spell out his name. Other 'sneaky' ways to get that first name is the label on the Sports Illustrated in the lobby, the label on that UPS package that was just delivered, the diploma on the wall etc. Be Sherlock Holmes while the customer in front of you is at the counter. Think of it as a game.

And what about that gatekeeper? To be honest with you, I don't have much problem getting past her. Partly because I say "Could you please tell Joe that Jonny from American Family is here" then break eye-contact, start reading the wall again, and literally 'expect' her to get Joe for you. Listen, I know that nothing works all the time, but this usually works, especially using the first name.

I'm sure you've gotten "What's this in regards to?", I usually mention that "I work for some of his neighbors and I just want to see if he wants me to stop by on Friday while I am in town..." That usually does it.

Remember, it's mostly a mindset. Nothing works all of the time, but really, if you think of this as a game, you can have a lot of fun with it.

Name dropping also adds credibility to what you do. If you are brand new, 'borrow' credibility. For instance, if 3 doors prior, Sally's widget shop said, "we already have Aflac", don't be discouraged, be thankful that you can borrow that credibility. Don't ever lie, but you can say to Ray at Ray's Repair, "Hey, you must be Ray. I haven't had a chance to meet you yet. I'm Jonny the Aflac guy, and 'we' work for a lot of your neighbors, like Sally at the widget factory. Unfortunately, I'm on the way to Manchester right now, but I am going to be back in town on Friday. Say, if I stop by with a brochure, could you give me 5 minutes so I can show you how Aflac works? You've seen the duck on TV right?"… Now you have used the power of his own name, added the credibility of his neighbor, and acted like you were in a real hurry. I'm telling you, he wants to do business with you, and he's not even sure what you do!

One more tip is that quite often the worker bees will lead you to the queen. Instead of going to the sales counter at that local garage, walk into one of the service bays. For starters, you just avoided the receptionist. Secondly, there is a good chance that you could catch the owner himself under a hood. But thirdly, you can ask the 'worker-bee' mechanic, "Are you the owner here sir?". Even when it is quite obvious he's not, this little bit of flattery often leads to, "No, its Pat inside, the big guy with the moustache", hence, your access to give the opening line to the owner, along with the power of knowing and saying his name.

Anything worth doing, is worth doing wrong a whole bunch of times until you get it right. Remember, as part of our success strategy, we are getting real good at what we do while focusing primarily on the smaller groups. One advantage is that you have a whole lot more access to that business owner, and besides, if you totally mess one up, you might have messed up on $200, but better than on an account that would have netted you $2500. But as part of this entire strategy, these small businesses are going to bridge you to the larger accounts.

One more thing to address, what about that 'No Soliciting' sign? Trust me, ignore it! Just walk right in like you own the place or like they should be expecting you. The huge advantage to that door is that they are not bombarded by sales reps, because most reps see that sign and move on. You are not selling him anything, but rather stopping by to introduce yourself, and let him or her know that you will be in town on Friday. In food sales we used to say that that sign was codeword for, "please don't stop here, my wife buys everything". And just like knowing their name ahead of time, they never mention the sign that you just walked by. But just like before, be in a hurry, talk quick, and get out of there.

5 Minutes with That
Business Owner

Okay, now we are back in town, about to walk into that small business, and get '5 minutes' with that busy business owner you gave your opening line to just days ago.

Remember to keep the mindset that you are about to show him the greatest thing since sliced bread. 'You' actually have a way for him to offer additional benefits to his employees, that doesn't cost him anything, and actually protects his own interests! You have something he needs, and something he is going to desperately want after just 5 minutes with you.

Right now, he really doesn't know what you do. He does remember however, (because we gave him that impression) that you are a very busy businessperson yourself, and that you (or other agents) already 'work' for some of his neighboring business owners.

Most likely, we were 'loosey-goosey' with the time you would pop in, rather than necessarily nailed down to a specific time. So, there is a chance that though he or she recognizes you, they may have to finish the immediate task or phone-call before giving you that '5 minutes'. That is fine, keep in mind that you are on their turf and need to be flexible, and their business comes first. But much more often than not, they will say something like, "Oh yeah 'Aflac right?' Okay, whatcha got?"

If they seem like they may be busy for quite awhile, don't twiddle your thumbs in that waiting room endlessly. It is critical to keep in mind that we must give off an aura that we are busy and in high demand business owners ourselves. At least look busy, make a cell phone call or two, make notes in your datebook, or rifle through some papers. If they look like they are honestly trying to get free for a moment, I will be fairly patient, but be looking very busy at the same time. If I get the impression that he is dealing with a moderate crisis, or there are 3 customers in line vying for his attention, then I will usually poke my head in and say (with a smile), that I apologize, but I have someone else that I need to meet with so I need to go, but that I will try to stop back by after, or perhaps later that afternoon. They actually appreciate your understanding and flexibility. Also, it adds to your credibility that you are busy, got places to go, and people to see.

Alright, let's assume he waves us into his office, and gives us the, "Whatcha got?" (He may even add something like, "you've got 5 minutes"). That's all good. Once we can get a business owner's undivided attention for 5 minutes, we can get our message across.

Now, you may be wondering how in the world this could ever transpire in just 5 minutes. Relax, I am going to show you that too. But if 5 minutes into it, he is totally on board, asks additional questions, or transitions into a lot of small talk, he gave us the time extension, rather than us going way over our window in which we promised to be brief.

Regardless of how well you think a business owner presentation goes however, remember this:

Unless you leave with a signed m-0138 and/or a scheduled time

to meet with and present to the employees, the meeting was not a success.

That's not to say that you might not in fact do business with them in the future, but it can require countless frustrating call-backs, follow-ups, and heartache. You can even transform from the person with something great to offer them into a real pest that 'keeps calling about that Aflac thing.'

I want to hear 2 things all day long:

1. "This kinda sounds too good to be true!"

2. And "How's Aflac make any money?"

If you are not hearing these two things again and again, in my opinion you need to tweak what you are saying out there.

I always respond to either of those responses with, "Yeah, I get that a lot" and then repeat the other question that they are also thinking.

This should sell itself, almost every single time!

Keep in mind, that many of these businesses are too small to offer any benefits (which may change w/Obamacare), and I am continually amazed how many employees, and even small business owners themselves, are totally without any medical insurance.

Now back to the actual presentation itself to that business owner, I have two words that sum up the effectiveness of getting our message across: **STORIES SELL!**

I start with a very brief, "Are you familiar with Aflac?" Usually you will get the, "Just the duck on TV"…

I start with a separating clause from the start, about how "Forbes rated us the #1 insurance company in the world, the year 'before' we had the duck. Then, how ingenious marketing has since bridged us to being the 2nd most recognized icon in America, next to the M &

M guys. But also how most people still really don't understand what exactly it is that we do, thus the reason for our 5 minutes together today."

Then I start with how "First of all, We are not 'health insurance'"_I then go on to say that "health insurance is important, but as you know, health insurance costs hundreds and hundreds of dollars a month, goes up every year, and then how they pay everybody 'else', like the doctors, hospitals, nurses, and x-ray centers etc. In contrast, most Aflac policies are about $5/week, have never gone up in prices since 1955, and we only send money to you, or your employee."

Remember, we are selling a concept. We need to paint a picture of how a sudden unexpected car accident for example could absolutely devastate that employee financially. I realize that we offer a lot more products than just the accident policy, and here is where I may differ from what you may have been taught or may be doing, but hear me out please. I also sell a ton of everything else from cancer to dental, but I 'drive home' the concept with the accident plan. And there are many times that in fact I will 'only' mention the accident plan, at least for now. Allow me to proceed with this and I think that you will be able to see where I am coming from. Remember, you can always up-sell, but if you overwhelm them at first, they may very well tune you out all together.

Okay, after my brief introduction, and the clause separating me from health insurance, I say, "We have a series of policies, but this one right here is by far our most popular one. It is called our 'accident and injury' plan. Let me show you how it works. If you get hurt at all doing virtually anything, 24/7, on the job or off the job, and have to go to the doctor, dentist, emergency room, chiropractor, or hospital, the first thing we do is give you $120, just for being looked at. This is supposed to kind of make up for you sitting in an emergency room or waiting room all day waiting to get an x-ray or stitches, when you could have been at work making money that day. But if it happened on a weekend or on a day that you weren't scheduled to work anyway, you still get the money. In fact we are the fastest paying company by far" (*then I point to the back of the brochure where it says, 'most claimed processed in 4 days'*) "As you know, worker's comp. or disability doesn't kick in until you miss at least a week of work. Again, you could get hurt playing softball, hurt your back shoveling snow, break a tooth on a piece of candy, cut your finger in the kitchen and need a few stitches... whatever"

Now I transition into a storyteller. Your actual benefit amounts may of course be slightly different in your state, but you will see how I get my point across. Also, although stories sell, remember at first I didn't have any of my own stories, so I borrowed them from other reps at first. Now I have my own, but there are still a few borrowed ones that are my favorites.

Okay, back to the 'script'. "But that's just for being looked at. From there all of these different injuries have a dollar value, from $35 for literally a paper-cut, to $12,500 for a major injury, like a 3rd degree burn, coma or an injury to your spine. All your body parts are numbered, and they match that body part number to the specific injury, and that's how they come up with a dollar value. It might sound kind of morbid, but that's how it works. Like fractures for example, if you have a hairline fracture in your pinkie-toe, its worth another $65. They are not going to do much for it, except maybe tape it to the next one. And you're not going to miss any work from it, you're going to take Advil and limp around for a couple days. But you'd get the $120 plus the $65, or $185. But that's for a pinkie-toe. But what this is really for, is like a company I just did Aflac for not too long ago in Pepperell, Mass. Just a week after their Aflac kicked in, one of the girls there was in a major car accident, fractured her hip and pelvis, and between her injury benefits, hospital, and rehab, she got $11,000! And it was in her mailbox just a little over a week from the time she got home from the hospital. In March, we gave a guy $1500 hundred dollars for a bad sunburn! He fell asleep on his honeymoon, naked, face-up! I have a radiator guy in New Hampshire who had a 3rd degree burn when the anti-freeze vat tipped over on him, literally scalding him and taking the skin right off! A 3rd degree burn pays $12,500. And then with cuts, like I said a paper-cut starts at $35, but then it goes up depending on the millimeters of stitches etc. For example, I did the Aflac for a pizza shop in Methuen, Mass, and somehow a kid there missed with the round cutter thing that they use, and it went up his hand

(I re-enact the injury with my hand motion). He got $775, and it was based on the amount of stitches he had and how many millimeters etc. Now he did miss one day of work, sitting in the emergency room all day with a bloody towel waiting to get sown up, but then he was able to go back to work, all bandaged up, and trying to be more careful. But what this is really there for though is if his hand had been aching too bad and he had to take a few days off, then the $775 really would have made a big difference, because your car payment is due whether you are working or not. And a couple weeks ago, a guy called me on his way to work, cuz while he was driving, he opened a bag of chips with his teeth, and his front tooth went flying (and I demonstrate the motions with my hands again), he got I think it was $330 towards his cap. And he wasn't about to go homeless, but he did spend all day in a dental lab when he could have been working."

Then I add my own personal story:

"The reason I am so passionate about this is that in 1999, a drunk driver ran me off the highway in Cape Cod, I rolled down an embankment in my delivery van, and I was out of work for about 6 months, and I did lose my house! They really do take your car at midnight! And it wasn't anything I did wrong. And even though the parents of the drunk kid who hit me owned the car and had insurance, and I eventually got a settlement, it was too late. It was almost 2 years later! I wish I had had Aflac then. I went from a large house to a 2nd floor apartment with 4 daughters stuffed into one bedroom with 2 sets of bunk-beds."

On top of that, if you are hurt bad enough that they have to admit you to the hospital, we know you are missing work, so that is where the bigger money kicks in. For that first overnight, you will get $1,250, and then keep getting $250/day while you are there, up to a whole year! Now hopefully you are never in the hospital for a whole year 'cuz you are pretty screwed up if you are, but at least you know that you are getting $7,500/month tax-free sent to the house so the bills are paid, so you can worry about getting better, not about whether or not your kids are gonna be homeless when you get out. If you are admitted to ICU, then the benefits are over twice that amount.

Now, even if it's not inpatient, there are also benefits for MRIs and CAT scans, rehab, follow-up visits, physical therapy etc. And the appliance benefit…A couple weeks ago, my daughter sprained her ankle in gym class. We got $70 for the pediatrician visit, and $125 for the 'appliance' benefit, because the doctor's note said, 'Sophie should use crutches.' So we got a check for $195. Now Sophie doesn't pay any of the bills at home, she's 12, but my wife teaches Pilates. But that day, she had to cancel all of her classes, pick up Sophie at school, take her to the doctor, and wait for an x-ray, so that $195 helped because my wife missed a day at work. Again, this is a benefit where it is different than disability, because as you know, disability can only cover 'you', not your family members and children. And even then, usually only after you miss at least a week of work.

It also pays for blood and plasma, prosthetics, there's more money for an ambulance ride, and transportation…We have a policy holder in Sanford, Maine, who's daughter was attacked and bitten in the face by a German shepherd and hurt pretty bad. She received a couple thousand dollars for the surgical procedure, hospital etc, but because the surgery had to be done in Boston, and they live near Portland, the mother got $600 from the 'transportation' benefit to cover her gas driving back and forth to Boston. Plus, we paid for Mom's hotel room. Again, those are expenses that health insurance can't address and usually comes right out of your pocket.

You don't want to think about losing fingers and toes and arms and legs, but it could happen, so there is dismemberment benefit. And then, God forbid you ever died in an accident, this plan also comes with $40,000 life insurance that you would leave to a named beneficiary.

Now anybody can get Aflac, and we write hundreds and hundreds of policies to individuals, but if you can get it through your work, it is usually about half price. And the best part…the employees gladly pay for this themselves, but you are the hero because you 'offered' Aflac at your company.

Then, if your employee ever leaves, they can take this with them, and they get to keep that half price rate!

Oh yeah, and claims…they call me. It's a 1 page claim form. If anything happens, they call me, I have them sign the bottom of it, I can fill out most of the rest, and then I put it in with their doctor's note, discharge papers, or whatever they have…and they should have their money in about a week. And no matter how many claims they have, we can't cancel them and are not going to go up on their rates.

As I whipped through everything I just said, I have an opened accident brochure in front of them, and am pointing from paragraph to paragraph as I am telling my stories.

Now comes a critical transition point, where you are going to slam home the sale, and set the stage for presenting to and enrolling the employees. At this point they should be totally on board and enthusiastic about what they just heard, and even skeptical about it being too good to be true. But now for the slam dunk…

"As a business owner, this also protects 'you'. As you know, and like they teach us in insurance school, almost 2 out of 3 worker's comp. claims are filed on Monday mornings at about 10:00, if you know what I mean." (And they 'always' know what I mean, and usually are nodding their head) "That guy who really hurt himself playing football on Sunday limps into work on Monday, and pretends that to get hurt lifting something off that top shelf…Not that they are all dishonest, but they are desperate. This alleviates a lot of that, because they know they have Aflac. Or, they assume that because you own a business, you are a millionaire and they ask you for a loan 'cuz they can't pay their rent, and that puts you in an awkward position because you have your own bills to pay. 'Now they have Aflac!'"

Okay, at this point you have rounded third base, and are sprinting to cross home, but if you don't get this next part down, you can very easily get thrown out at the plate, or at least be stranded at third base for a very, very long time.

Your mindset has to be that of a 'consultant' more than just a salesperson. That business owner doesn't necessarily know his 'lines' yet, so we must take the lead on what happens next.

The two big concerns or thoughts that may be in his or her mind are:

1. Can my employees afford even $5/week?

2. Am I going to have to shut down operations and lose production for a day if we do this?

Let's beat him to the punch, and answer his questions before he even thinks to ask them.

The most powerful phrase that closes the deal I learned from my friend Noella, also a district in my region. That phrase, **"The next step is…"** Remember, that business owner doesn't know what the next step is, or is supposed to be, so we need to tell them, or *lead* them.

"Now, Mr. business owner, would you say that this is better than you thought it might be, or did you really have no idea just what we do?"

You should get some kind of, "Yeah, it sounds pretty good. Can I get this for myself?" or "It kind of sounds too good to be true."

My response, "Yeah, I get that a lot, but I do the claims and they really are that good. Even though I am in the insurance business, in my opinion, most companies try to find a way 'not' to pay claims. But Aflac really is different. They 'get it'." They understand that by being known as the best paying company out there, people talk, and that's why they get that A+ rating year after year that is coveted in the insurance industry" (and I point to the A+ rating cited on the back of the brochure).

"Now the next step is…, first (pointing to myself) I have to apply for an exact industry rating for your company. They 'rate' your business based on how dangerous an industry you are in. It's usually somewhere between $4 and $10/week. Your employees don't all have chainsaws in their hands atop ladders, so it should come back around $5 or $6/week, like I said. That will take me a couple of days. Then the next step is… When's the best time of day we could get most of your employees together, just for like 5 to 10 minutes, so I could explain how Aflac works? 'Very similar to what I just did with you, except a little more fun because I bring a talking duck with me. But what's the best time we could get most of them together, just for like 5 minutes, so I can explain how it works, then send them all back to work, but see what kind of response we get?" Then I might suggest, "first thing in the morning before the drivers hit the road, or maybe a 10:00 break?"

If they answer that question, you're coming in to sell Aflac that day!

If they say probably first thing in the morning, around 10:00 break, I reply, "Perfect. I am booked about a week out," (again subtly reminding them I am in high demand, and that a whole lot of other businesses are 'doing it'), "but next week I could do 5 minutes or so around 10:00 on either Tuesday or Wednesday." I've pulled out and opened my datebook, which is extremely full of appointments and notes, clicked my pen, and hovered over next week's slots, waiting to jot down his business in either the Tuesday or Wednesday square.

Note: If your datebook doesn't look like a field of chicken-scratch full of appointments, then for now fill all the squares with, 'walk the dog', 'date night', 'cold calling', 'haircut', 'whatever'. You need to look extremely busy. "Fake it 'til you make it".

His line, "Yeah, probably Tuesday I guess."

CLOSED!

"Excellent", (then I add) "you probably don't want to even try to explain this to them between now and then, because they won't really 'get it'. As soon as you mention the insurance word, they'll tune you out, and either think that it is health insurance, or that they could never afford it. But it has been my experience that whenever I can explain it to people, within 5 minutes or so, 90% of people 'get it'. The only place I haven't gotten that response was once at a Chinese restaurant in Manchester, and they had no idea what I was saying (true story). "Or, maybe if they're 18, still live at home, and if they get hurt it doesn't really matter because they won't be homeless anyway. But when I talk to adults, it is totally voluntary, but almost everybody gets it."

GETTING THE M-0138 SIGNED

You need to very much make this not a big deal at all. I give the impression that they are not so much 'signing a contract' as much they are applying for an industry rating, and allowing me to set up his business with the ability to bring in Aflac, if there is in fact a positive response from the employees.

I say, "Do you have a card?" or "Is this basic information on your card current?" I have written the name of his business on page 1 in front of him. Holding his card in my left hand, I say "This is pretty much all I need to get that rate for you, and most of this I can fill out later." Then I ask, "Oh, do your employees get paid weekly or every other? 'Cuz I am supposed to be able to give them a 'per-pay-period' quote when I come back."

The employer: "Yeah, every Friday."

I then put a line through sections 4, 5, and 6 while I am still in front of him, regarding pre-taxing. Possibly muttering, "We can skip all this and keep it simple." Then I get to where he or she signs and say, "Alright…again, you're not getting insurance today, you are just requesting for me to get you a rate, and set things up so that if your employees do in fact want this when I come back, they can get it. Also, this insures that this will never cost you a dime." (Of course, slightly larger companies may pre-tax, but I am keeping it as simple as possible, assuming that this is a garage or salon where they don't offer any kind of benefits.)

Hand him the pen.

Body language is everything, and so is the mindset. Expect him to sign it, and really, why wouldn't he? This costs him nothing, and could very well protect him as a business owner. But, don't say a word once you hand him the pen until he either signs it, or has a question, (even if 40 seconds goes by).

Next, you take it from him and say, "Thanks so much for your time today." He almost always thanks you back as well.

Now that you've closed the deal, continue to give the impression that you've got to get to another appointment. Be closing your folder, putting your datebook back in your bag or whatever, but 'now' you find a way to bond with him, even if it's something minor.

Look for something on the wall, or a picture on his desk. Find 'some' common ground, anything you can relate to. If you see a picture of a boy in a hockey uniform, and you've been a hockey dad, make small talk about it. "Is that your son? Who's he play for? This was my first year as a hockey dad with the 5am practices..." Or, if there is a picture of him holding a salmon in a river, "Wow, is that a salmon? I love to fish but I've never caught one of those, that must be a rush!..." Or, (especially in the Boston market) if there is a sports team displayed, chances are that they are a 'passionate' fan. "Have you been to any games this year?" or "How about Big Papi, with two more homers last night."

Now, if they talk about their kid, big catch, or favorite team, for 10 minutes even, let them! The more you let them talk about one of their passions, the more they will start to like you. It's weird but it works. I don't know much about classic cars, but if they have 3 pictures plus a calendar of custom Corvettes on the wall, I'll ask them something about it. Their passion could be dogs, weight lifting, boating...whatever. Get them to talk about it and they will like 'you'.

Leave with direct eye contact, a firm handshake, and a smile saying, "Thanks again, I look forward to seeing you Tuesday."

Don't act too excited 'til you get in the car. Then you can call your

DSC with the good news, or scream "Yee-haw!" out the window and slap the dashboard.

This process takes practice, but it is worth getting right. You will become a machine, giving this presentation to 10 small business owners a week.

Remember our game plan? We talked about getting 4 out of 10 business owners to say yes. Believe it or not, you will get 'much' better than that. I've had many weeks where I was 9 for 10, or even 10 for 10.

Remember my associate Tim? He holds our district record, getting 6 m-1's signed in a day. 4 in a day has been done several times, by 3 different associates. And our district is only 6 months old!

A couple of variables:

If actually nailing down a time to meet with the employees is a challenge, 'help' him figure it out. One thing I suggest when this is the case, or if several people have scattered shifts, is coinciding with an already scheduled meeting. For example, many companies have a mandatory meeting once a week or once a month. Others have a 'safety' meeting. Perhaps there is another reason for the employees assembling after closing time etc. I've done this successfully with teachers, police officers, highway departments, fire stations, restaurants, nurses, real estate offices etc. If they are getting together anyway, you have a captive audience. I do suggest however that I go first at the meeting. That way people don't disappear like cockroaches once the meeting is over and the 'insurance guy' wants to talk to everybody. This is one area where you need to be flexible. Sometimes it's best to catch the drivers at 7am before they start making their deliveries. I've even enrolled police officers on the midnight shift. It is rare that I am working other than the hours of 8:30 to 3:30, but if I am, I'm making money, because access to the employees is where we cash in.

What you visualize and focus on 'will' come to pass. So, expectantly create a scenario in your mind. Picture that delighted business owner ecstatic after your 5- minute presentation with him. Picture him signing the m-1 and scheduling you in right away to meet with his employees.

Self talk needs to be positive, not fearful. Say to yourself (even out loud) what you want to happen. 'Don't' let yourself express your fears out loud, or envision them. Telling a child, "Walk" and "Don't run" is NOT the same thing. What you hear is what you visualize, and what you visualize in your mind usually comes to pass. When that child hears "run" he doesn't hear the "don't". If you say, "walk", that's what they picture too.

Similarly, don't say (or think), "I hope the secretary doesn't stop me" or "I hope the business owner doesn't want to talk to his employees first before I have a chance to" or "I hope the enrollment doesn't get rescheduled".

Instead, replace that with, "I can't wait to make that secretary's day" and "that business owner is going to love this whole thing" and "I can't wait to present this to the employees, I'm gonna make a lot of money on this one".

Lastly, remember that you are on par with that business owner. Don't be intimidated. You're a business owner, and he's a business owner. You're busy and so is he. Relate to him as a fellow entrepreneur that you are going to do business with. This positions you less as a salesman, and more as an associating professional.

One note to those of you who are wondering when you get to mention the other products you can sell. This is always a judgment call, and when in doubt, I want to err on the side of keeping it simple and writing business, rather than overwhelm the whole concept, and blow the whole deal. Depending on the industry, there are many times that I will 'only' mention the accident plan during those 5 minutes with the business owner, then I will up-sell them at the laptop. (I will address this in a later chapter). That employer may very well picture his employees spending $5/week after hearing your stories, but if you overwhelm him with cancer, specified health, accident and hospital plans, and then you also mention life, dental, vision, and family plans... if he perceives $38/week as totally out-of-the-budget for Jonny Lunch-bucket, he won't even let you near his workers. He's 'protecting' them. Yet, I can't tell you how many times I got to the employee presentation, 'then' added on a cancer product at the end of it. Sometimes the up-sell is just done at the laptop.

Think of it like a haircut. When the haircut is over, if you think it's not short enough yet, you can always cut off more. But if you go too far from the start, it's too late.

Just focus on the accident for now, and get a bunch of businesses closed, and get paid. As your confidence grows, then I would suggest talking to that employer about accident and cancer, how, "We specialize in protecting against the 2 most likely events that can devastate a family financially, a terrible accident, or a bout with cancer..."

At the time of this writing, I have also had the privilege of working with another up-and-coming rookie sensation, John Amero. John was a friend of mine before I was ever in Aflac, and had wanted the accident protection for his own contracting business. I recruited him, and he has made himself absolutely teachable from the beginning. He has followed my system to the 'T', and the results have been amazing. He didn't waste any energy questioning the system, but believed in it, and ran with it. In just his second full quarter in the business, he closed out quarter 3, 2010 (13 weeks) with an applaudable 23 new accounts, writing over 200 policies for over $79,000 AP. I have a feeling that he is just getting started.

Just one more thing, then I promise we will get to the employees. Many times I am running my 5-minute presentation with a business owner who has actually heard an Aflac presentation before. Some have seen it a few times. I am repeatedly told that I explain it 'so much better'. It's because of the stories! I do kept it simpler, but I am getting the concept across with the accident brochure, and they 'get it' when they hear the stories. Don't put them to sleep reading a brochure, bring the policy to life with real life examples more than anything else you do.

CHAPTER RECAP

- Keep it Simple
- Be a story teller
- Remember, "The next step is…"
- Visualize your desired outcome
- Remember your objective: See the employees!
- Bond with that business owner 'after' your presentation

The Employee Presentation and Enrollment

Okay, it's 9:45, and we are on the way to see the workers at XYZ Repair shop. Today is payday, where we are going to present to the employees and enroll them.

Visualize what your desired outcome is. Decide what you want to happen, and even write down your goal.

If it's a small garage with just an owner and two mechanics:

I would like to write 3 accident policies 'today', and close this account, making over $200.

If it's a slightly larger company, and you know there are 5 techs, 1 secretary, plus the owner:

I would like to write at least 10 policies to at least 5 employees 'today' and make over $700.

It doesn't matter where you write it down. I've done it on a napkin right before a presentation. But the actual process of writing down what you would like to happen clarifies your desired outcome, and I believe 'sets the table' before you even arrive. If you've never heard of doing such a thing, I challenge you to try it for 30 days prior to every employee presentation, and see the results for yourself. It's a powerful tool that the super-successful over-achievers in many industries use to clarify their desired outcomes.

Okay, hopefully that employer gathers the worker-bees for you, and you have their undivided attention, even if it's only for a few minutes. You may have to be patient and wait for Sally or Johnny to come back from a delivery, finish with a customer, or cash out a ticket, but start as close to 'on-time' as possible. It is critical that you maximize and take advantage of this opportunity, yet at the same time be respectful of the fact that more often than not, they are 'on the clock', so time is money (literally). The advantage to presenting while on the clock is that usually they will gladly take a 'paid break' to hear what you have to say, even if they don't think that they would be interested.

You want to start with a captivating introduction, a defined ending with specific instructions at the close, and in between, several stories that take the group through a roller coaster of emotions within just a few minutes.

For an introduction, I say, "Good morning everybody. Who here is already familiar with Aflac?" Almost every hand goes up. (That quickly you just got the audience to participate). You usually hear, "The duck on TV, everyone's seen the duck."

My response, "Yup, everyone's seen the duck, but other than knowing that it is some kind of insurance, most people don't really know just what it is we do. Is that fair to say?" You get several nods, again...audience participation.

"Well in fact, our spokesperson insisted on coming today." Then you put a talking duck on the table, press the button, and every eye goes to it, and you get a room full of "Aaaww's" and laughs from the employees. (You've just broken down several walls of resistance because you've already connected with their emotions.)

Then I get right into, "Aflac is not health insurance. Health insurance is important, but as you know it costs hundreds of dollars a month, goes up every year, and their job is to pay everybody else, the doctors, hospitals, x-ray centers, nurses etc. Most Aflac policies are about $5/week, and we haven't raised our rates since 1955. And we send money to 'you'."

"We have a series of policies, but this one right here is by far our most famous", (holding up the accident brochure). "If you've ever seen the commercial where a guy has his leg up on the table in a cast while the duck is mailing out bills...well that's the message we are trying to get across. If you get hurt, doing pretty much anything, we are going to send you cash, which 'Is just as good as money' as Yogi put it."

At this point I am cruising, have already emotionally connected with the audience thanks to the talking duck, and the '$5/week' has peaked their curiosity. Now for the roller coaster of emotions...

For the most part, the next couple minutes of telling stories while going through the accident brochure is 'identical' to the pitch I gave to the owner. The effect is only multiplied because of the reactions and facial expressions going around the room as I tell the stories. Even though the claim is a year and a half old, and it's not even mine, I 'always' use the $1500 to the naked, face-up, honeymooner sunburn, because it gets a lot of 'ooohs', 'ows' contorted faces, and laughs from the crowd.

Again, the presentation itself is the same one as in the previous chapter given to the employer, but we do have a different close...

As I complete going through the brochure and telling my stories, I close with the accidental death life insurance (and wellness if it applies in that state), then I ask, "Are there any questions so far?" If there is one, I always say, "Great question." Complimenting them on being so smart, they are usually the first customer after the meeting. I answer the questions as they come. If there aren't any, I go for the close.

Usually one of the questions is "How do you guys make any money?" Then several other people chime in, "I was wondering the same thing."

Occasionally, nobody asks it, even though they are all thinking it, so I will volunteer, "One question I do get a lot is, 'How do you guys make any money?'…" and you get a lot of nods across the room. Now you explain, "Aflac has both the smallest profit margin and the largest customer base. It's called the law of large numbers. For every dollar that comes in, almost 71 cents goes out the same day to pay a claim. This is by far the smallest margin in the industry, but with so many millions of American's paying in between $5 to $10/week, its there when one of us needs it. They have $84 billion in assets, so they don't need a bailout, or a buy-out, or aren't going to take a dive like an AIG. And that's just here, in Japan, 1 in 4 people already has Aflac. And they already have their own national health care. But they understand that this doesn't go to the doctors…Aflac is to pay the rent." Now you have their interest and their trust.

I close with, "A couple legalese things…" (pointing to the back of the brochure) "You can't 'intentionally' inflict injury to collect Aflac money," (Say it with a smile and you get one more laugh from the audience), "It has to at least 'look' like an accident… And you can't be in the act of committing a felony when you get hurt, like getting shot by the cops after robbing a bank, they probably won't pay that claim. But you 'can' be mountain biking, roller skating, skiing, and I even own a cage-fighting school. They will pay the claims every single time. And we won't go up on your rate or cancel you because you have a claim."

Then I add, "Oh by the way, if you find yourself in the emergency room waiting for a stitch or an x-ray, and the lady with the clipboard asks, "Do you have any 'other' insurance you want to tell us about?" This is a "No." You are not being un-ethical for not disclosing this.

This is not other 'health' insurance, this is like your own 'paycheck' insurance. Our stance isn't that if you owe the hospital, not to pay them. But we know that if times got really tight because of a car accident like I had where I was out of work for six months, that hospital would take $50/month for the next 5 years, but your landlord won't, the mortgage company won't, your car payment won't, the light bill or the grocery store. If you want to use Aflac money to cover a deductible, you decide that, but it is going to go through your hands first. And no, you will not get in trouble if you use Aflac money to go on a cruise. In fact you might just get better faster if you were in the Bahamas."

"Again, this is our most popular plan, and about 65 million Americans already have it. Anyone in the world can get Aflac, and we write hundreds of individual policies, and that runs somewhere around $61/month (quoting a direct family plan), but because Mr. Smith (the business owner) is offering this here at work, you guys get this for $6.02/week! (example: NH c-rate) And its not $6 for everybody in the house, its only like a dollar-something to add a spouse, I think around 9 bucks is the whole family plan. And if you ever leave this company, whether its 10 weeks from now or 10 years, you get to take this with you, and it stays 6 bucks a week!"

Now it is critical that you conclude your presentation with very specific instructions. Remember that they don't know how this works, so we need to tell them. I conclude with, "Alright, thank you everybody for your time. I will be parked over there in the corner office after this. Anyone who wants Aflac, it takes a couple minutes with me entering you into the laptop. I just need a date of birth, the address you want checks mailed to, and a named beneficiary for the life insurance that comes with it. I want to be sensitive to anyone that needs to go first because they have an appointment or need to meet a customer, or need to leave for a delivery or something. Does anybody need to go first?" This starts the stampede, and people actually vie for an opportunity to go first.

My regional Bill Henry says that golden rule #1 in any sales is 'Make it easy for them to get whatever it is you're selling.' Keep this process simple, low key, and expect everyone to enroll. For five bucks, why would anybody not?

Occasionally you may get a, "Do I have to decide today?" or "Can I check with my husband first?" I keep it real low key, and answer, "Absolutely, I understand. This is 100% voluntary. There is no pressure to sign up for anything. But if you think you 'may' want to take advantage of getting Aflac half price, then we can just capture your information, put it 'on-hold', and as long as I witness you picking a beneficiary in front of me and I can witness a signature for that, we can do the rest over the phone. If in two days you call me and decide you don't want Aflac, I just simply remove you from my data base. If you call me and decide you do, I simply put your application in with all the others, but that way we don't have to meet again. And that's not to say that if you decide a year from now that you want it, we could always do it then, but between now and then the chances of me getting back here within the next few months could be tough, because I am already scheduled to work for dozens of companies over the next several weeks."

This is my 'take-away' close. Quite simply, if they want Aflac, I'm here today. My time is much too valuable to do this more than once. I did act like this from the very beginning. Today, it is an absolute reality. One auto-body in Hudson, NH rescheduled their initial enrollment over a year and a half ago (it was the second m-0138 I ever got signed). Recently the owner called me and said, "Hey Jonny, you still doing Aflac, cuz we're ready now." My reply, "Sure Dave, great to hear from you. It will be a month or more before I can get to you though, I'm booked out pretty far..." That was a great feeling to be able to tell him that, and I meant it!

I do realize that an awful lot of Aflac agents present to the employees on one day, and then come back several days later to actually do the enrollment. I will 'never' run my business that way. My time is much too valuable to run the same location twice like that. I feel I can be twice as effective and efficient by working smarter, and maximizing my time. If you are doing things differently yet you are satisfied with the results, by all means, don't change a thing. But, if you want to move into 'rapid-fire' mode, consider my thought process on this. I am definitely not saying that my way is the only way, but rather that this machine-gun approach has been working extremely well for our region, and we are constantly breaking records.

The response has been phenomenal, and most often we get 90 to 100% participation from the employees.

Once the enrollment process is completed, remind the secretary or the owner how 'simple' the billing system works, and reassure them that you will be in contact soon to drop off the deduction report. Thank them one more time for allowing you to offer Aflac to their employees. After that, stay in touch periodically. You become like a rock-star over time as you stay in contact with the account and service their claims.

Chapter Recap

- Get audience participation by asking questions and by introducing the duck
- Take them through a roller-coaster of emotions by telling stories
- Make it easy for them to "Get it"
- Close with specific instructions
- Visualize your desired outcome

THE UPSELL

The cash register is rolling and making that "ka-ching" sound when that employee is sitting with you at the laptop. Every step of the system has led up to this moment: that worker signing up for Aflac.

Now I am fairly healthy and for the most part try to eat relatively healthy, but more often than I like, I find myself in a local McDonald's. It's not because it's my favorite food, but because they usually have WIFI, so throughout the day, after each enrollment, my team and I like to transmit our business right away. So a little too often, I end up getting something to eat there.

I've noticed that even the lowest-level cashier has been trained to up-sell. "Would you like fries with that?" or "Would you like cheese on that?"

Now, if everybody we see just buys an accident policy from us, we are still going to make a lot of money, but lets see if we can 'super-size' a few orders.

Obviously, if you have presented more than just accident, perhaps cancer, specified health, or disability, there is an opportunity to up-sell. But let's go back to our rapid-fire '3 accidents-and-out' enrollments at all of the mom and pop garages etc., and 'offer some fries with that'.

Allow me to show you 4 classic but subtle up-sells.

1) The 'NIGHT CRAWLER'

The easiest way is what I call the 'night crawler'. If you fish at all, you know that it is a popular bait that you can toss out there, and you just never know what might bite on to it.

After enrolling that employee on the accident plan, I pretend we are done, but say, "Thanks again. Remember to be careful 'til the first of the month because that's when your coverage starts…(in a joking tone of voice)… Also, don't forget that now that you guys here all have a group in place, keep us in mind if anyone ever has a need for dental insurance, life, or vision. 'Cuz now that you have a group in place, you will always get discounted group rates on any those in the future as well…"

I can't tell you how many times I've gotten the response, "You guys have dental? How much is that?"

My response, "Like I mentioned, most of our plans are between $5 to $10 a week. Let me check, do you need some work done?…" Many times, it results in another sale. Mentioning it is a casual 'after-thought'. It's very low-key and very low-pressure, but even a couple up-sells like that a week can significantly boost your income. It doesn't have to be, and shouldn't be, a hard-sell. You are just throwing out a bait, and who knows, you might just catch something. I also get calls a month or two down the road from people who later get dental, but it's all because I threw out the bait while I was at the laptop.

2) 'RENT' (disability rider)

If your state has a disability rider attached to the accident plan, even 'Jonny lunch-bucket' may be up-sold a dollar or two.

As I am entering their initial information at the laptop, assuming the '3 accidents-and-out' account, I say to that mechanic, "Would you just want the basic coverage, or would you like to know what it would be to have your rent paid for a year as well if you got hurt and couldn't work?"

"How's that work?"

"Everything I told you guys about the accident plan is paid in lump sums, and can really pay significant money as it is, but some people want to know that on top of that, their most expensive bill (usually their rent) would be paid for a year if they got hurt and couldn't work."

If this 'night crawler' peaks their interest, price it with and without the rider, asking how much their rent (or mortgage) is. If their rent is say $900/month, an accident disability rider attached to the basic accident plan is probably only about $2/week more. If they flinch even at that, drop the subject, take the sale for just accident, and be sure to make them feel good about the protection they do have with it, but if they do bite, even a few of those a week or month adds to your income.

3) Hospital (for maternity)

If at a group, a guy is wondering about "What if my wife has a baby?" Obviously that's not an accident, and even disability on a spouse is limited, but a perfect 'fill' for this situation is the Hospital Plan, where it is available.

Using Plan I, with the initial hospital annual rider of $1000, in total his wife will probably get about $2000 for two nights in the hospital for a vaginal birth, and probably $3500 if a c-section requires five nights.

<u>2 nights for vaginal birth</u>

Initial hospitalization benefit	$1000
2 days @ $400/day 'sickness'	$ 800
2 days @ $100/day annual	$ 200
	$2000

5 nights for c-section

Initial hospitalization benefit	$1000
5 days @ 400/day 'sickness'	$2000
5 days @ $100/day annual	$ 500
	$3500

If the wife makes about $500/week, but wants to be home for 6 weeks after Junior is born, either scenario takes a lot of pressure off because of missed work.

Even if she had disability, she would get nothing for week one, and 'maybe' $300 for weeks two through six, equaling about $1500.

If this fills a need, you may very well be able to sell it.

4) **LIFE INSURANCE**

Our state training coordinator, Jennifer Henry, is the master of the, "Would you like fries with that?" At the laptop, prior to the enrollment, asks, "By the way, how are you doing for life insurance?" No matter what they answer... "that sounds like something that's important to you, we can talk about that after..." 'MASTERFUL!'

If they said, "I don't have any"...same answer

If they said, "I'm not sure" ...same answer

If they said, "I've got $250,000 on me and my wife" ...same answer

After the accident policy is signed, "Oh yeah, let me get you a quick price on that life insurance we talked about"

She has sold a lot of extra 'fries' that way.

My caution on all of these is to make sure to keep it simple. Feel good about any group you slam '3-accidents-and-out' even, but just subtly drop the bait while you are doing your thing, and even occasional up-sells can dramatically increase your income.

GET THAT REFERRAL!
(THE OTHER 'MAGIC LINE')

I don't know about you, but I've always felt awkward asking for a referral. For some reason, it didn't come natural to ask someone to help me.

Perhaps it's because I've been hesitant when that multi-level guy, vacuum guy, or even life insurance guy has asked me for a couple of names. It's not that I didn't want to help them, but the scenario in my own mind was that my friends and family would resent my sending a salesman their way.

But somehow, by not asking for referrals myself, I knew I was missing out on a valuable asset. In my prior food sales position, most of my referrals came to me unsolicited. People would occasionally just offer me a name, or the referred friend would actually seek me out. One thing was certain, these 'warm calls' were so much easier than cold calls, and the closing ratio was probably well over 90%.

When I entered the Aflac world, my mentor (Regional/ Bill Henry) told me that he had done about 300 cold calls at the start of his own Aflac career, but from then on, **never made a cold call again!** He works 100% off of referrals, and has a decade of 6-figure income results to prove it worked.

I listened!

He told me how he asked for them, and it totally clicked with me. I may have tweaked it a tiny bit, but all the credit rightfully goes to Bill on this one. It works!

I've asked other associates how they ask for referrals, and I usually get something like, "Can you give me some names of some business owners who's employees might be interested in Aflac..." Even though some business owners will respond to such a request, recognizing and appreciating an entrepreneur building a business, it still seems a little choppy to me.

But listen to this one...

Timing is everything, and for optimal results imagine citing this at the close of a successful enrollment where the small business owner was very impressed at the overwhelming response of his own employees enrolling in Aflac. Now you thank him one more time for allowing you to come in, but then you add...

"One more thing Mr. Jones, ... Who do you know that owns a business, that if I mentioned your name, they'd at least take a brochure from me?"

Read that again. Then read it again, and realize how non-confrontational that is. You're not asking for a 'list of names' of people to go and bug, but rather 'a' name of someone he knows. And even then, "Just to take a brochure from me".

My experience is that a particular name comes right out of their mouth. Their golfing partner, a close associate, a former employer... someone 'close' to them rolls right off of their tongue. And anyone that close to them is very responsive.

The results have been nothing short of incredible. The results: dangerously close to 100%.

Now if you've been applying the system in this book up to now, and you are closing say two to five groups a week on average, that's two to five very qualified referrals that are going to end up as new groups enrolled, most often within the same month. And coming from a referral, the enrollment conditions are even better.

You remember our activity plan of booking 10 appointments a week right? Well now at least a couple of those are already done for you.

I usually still like to do my opening line in person however, and it goes something like this... "Hi, you must be Marty. I'm Jonny the Aflac guy. I just did some work for Steve over at ABC Auto Parts, and he asked me to stop by and show you what I do. Unfortunately I am on the way to Manchester right now, but I am going to be back in town on Friday. Say, if I stop by in the Friday morning with a brochure, can you give me five minutes to show you what I did for Steve? You've seen the duck on TV right?"

The same dynamic is there from the 'magic' opening line as before, but now I'm doing Steve a favor by stopping by to help Marty. I'm telling you, Marty can't say no, because Steve sent me.

It works like a charm!

As with the rest of the system, it's worth practicing over and over until you get it right. I'm not even two years old in the business yet, and I've got a blue spiral-bound notebook 'full' of referrals. Many of the names are over a year old.

One other thing to mention, Steve often refers you to the owner of a business, slightly larger than his own. Then Marty's referral is to an even larger company. Progressively, your referrals start to get you into bigger and bigger accounts.

Now I may be unique, but to me it's a little bit like shooting fish in a bucket. I love the thrill of the game of cold calling, but I literally have so many referrals, I rarely have time to actually cold call. But the results (and the payday) are fantastic, so I am not about to stop.

Ready to take it to another level?

How about asking every 'employee' you enroll, right after you've filled out their PDA and shaken their hand, "By the way, who do you know that owns a business, that if I mentioned your name, they'd at least take a brochure from me?"

I've been amazed at some of the connections I've made from some of the lowest-level employees (waitresses, mechanics, warehouse) because their father, brother, or best friend's mother owns that factory, restaurant, pharmacy, etc. across town. With our fast track system laid out in the first few chapters, you should be averaging enrolling 16 employees a week. That's a whole lot of referrals. If every third employee gave you a decent lead, plus each business owner, you'll never be able to keep up with the warm calls!

BECOME A SPECIALIST

I know that one concern among new agents in Aflac, is whether or not their particular area has been 'saturated'. This, as is every other aspect of sales, is really a mental barrier, and is not an actual fact.

There may very well be a few 'typical' manufacturing companies, on Main St. USA, that have been bombarded by numerous anxious Aflac agents just doing their job. Geographically or demographically, they seem to be the perfect cookie-cutter Aflac account, 'perfect' for what we have to offer.

Wrap your mind around this... 'There are less than 500,000 Aflac accounts nation-wide, and MILLIONS of small businesses!' There are also tens of thousands of school systems and municipalities yet to be enrolled. Then there are also tens of millions of individuals who can get direct plans...

It's like the mosquito in a nudist colony, 'You can start anywhere!'

Even in Japan, where there really is an actual 25% market penetration, that still means that 75% of businesses there don't have Aflac yet!

Even if a company has been called on by a previous rep, "They haven't heard it 'til they've heard it from me!" (ie. Heard me tell my stories)

Just like the nay-sayers that whine that "Its so hard in this economy where there is 10% unemployment." To me that's good news, because that means that 90% of Americans ARE employed. That's more than enough for all of us to make our millions. You can either make excuses or money…you decide!

That being said, some insist that certain 'regions' are better. Just to debunk that thought, I've got to tell you a quick road story. 10 months into the business, my kids wanted to go to Disney. We had just bought a 23' camper, so we took a family 'business trip'. We did camp at Fort Wilderness inside Disney, and spent several days at the parks, but I also got my license in Florida prior to going down there, and told my wife Michelle that I planned to work a day or two down there. I did enroll an RV dealership and made $1500+ in a day! The kicker (I'm no geography expert, but Florida is next to Georgia, where HQ is), nobody there had a clue what Aflac was about, other than seeing the commercials! Just like back in New Hampshire. And…my 'business trip' (vacation) was tax deductible. Only in America! Only with Aflac!

But, just to set your mind free, this chapter is on becoming a specialist.

There are so many industries that are 'perfect' for Aflac. Once you've enrolled a few companies in a similar field, you can become a specialist in providing Aflac to that particular type of business.

Here are a few examples of businesses one could certainly 'specialize' in:

Daycares
Autobody/Garages
Real Estate Offices
Fire Departments

Restaurants

Car Dealerships

Hair Salons

Retail Shops

Fitness Studios

Veterinarians

Dentist Offices

Lawyers

Chiropractors

Pharmacies

These are just a few examples...

If your DSC assigned you to be 'the' rep in your state to offer Aflac to say RESTAURANTS in your area, you could retire 25 years from now, have made your millions, and still wouldn't have gotten to them all. You could break it down even more to just PIZZA RESTAURANTS. You'd still be busy for years to come. Think about the city you live in, how many pizza shops are there? Even small towns have a few. A city could easily have hundreds.

Whatever the industry, you can actually incorporate it into your opening line, "You must be Joe. I haven't had a chance to meet you yet. I'm Jonny the Aflac guy. I do a lot of work for the restaurant industry across the state. Unfortunately I'm on the way to Bedford right now, but I'm going to be back in town Friday morning. Say, if I stop by with a brochure, can you give 5 minutes? You've seen the duck on TV right?"

It creates momentum at the very start, and you actually bring credibility to yourself by being the industry 'expert' or specialist.

This is 90% mental, but if it helps open your mind, then it can propel you to greatness.

Furthermore, your referrals may very well be within the same industry. After enrolling a hair salon, you can ask the owner on the way out, "Thanks again Sarah, and oh one more thing... Who else do you know that owns a salon that if I mention your name would at least take a brochure from me?"

One dentist knows another, dealers know other dealers, mechanics know each other, etc. etc. etc.

In your nearest city, or within a few towns around you, there are literally dozens and dozens, if not hundreds, of each of the above categories that don't have Aflac!

My background being martial arts, there are literally hundreds of karate, judo, kung fu studios around. And that's just one aspect of the fitness world.

Again, if you could 'only' target one industry, it might actually be easier to wrap your brain around the endless opportunities out there. I just so happen to 'specialize' in several industries at the same time.

Have fun with this. Designate yourself an industry expert or specialist.

If you are a coordinator, you may even consider 'designating' your agents to become specialists. You could run a contest on most groups within their new field of expertise.

Have fun with it, the possibilities are truly endless.

THE 1-2 PUNCH

Once you truly comprehend the importance of getting the 'concept' across by telling stories throughout the accident brochure, there will come a time when you will be confident enough to present 2, or perhaps even 3 products, still within a 5 to 10 minute quickie with that business owner.

Still, always be willing to close '3 accidents and out', and realize you could make a fortune if there was in fact nothing else, but now lets present a 1-2 punch.

After my 5 minutes, my main objective is still to book a time to get in front of those employees and tell my stories. Sometimes I will just add, "Again, this is our most popular policy, but when I come back, if one or two of your employees wants information on the 'get sick' version of Aflac, I will have brochures with me for that as well..." Without even showing him or her an actual brochure, I have just set the table for a 1-2 punch, probably accident & cancer, or accident & sickness.

In my experience, if the employees are making less than say $12/ hour, more than a 2-plan offering tunes them out, and you just lost the opportunity to make hundreds of dollars with the 'accidents and out' mindset. Similar to the chapter on up-selling at the laptop, this needs to be very subtle, and not the aura of you 'overselling'.

One of my agents has found a niche with daycares, and the 1-2 punch of accident and sickness has worked out extremely well. My presentation in front of the employees (usually during 'nap-time' hour) is still identical right up to the close. After setting the expectation of the enrolling process ("I'll be set up over in that corner with my laptop for you guys to come over one at a time") I add, almost as an afterthought… "By the way, recently at ABC daycare in the next town over, some of the girls there asked about the 'get sick' version, especially if they may be planning to have a baby in the near future and would like a couple thousand dollars to stay home with the baby for a few weeks. If any of you want info on that, I have brochures on that too. That one is priced by your date of birth, 'age-banded', but it averages maybe $9/week…"

If it is appropriate to actually present the 1-2 punch in front of the group of employees together, I give a 1-minute commercial with the sickness brochure open in front of me (in states where PSI is available). I start with, "Okay everything we just talked about from hurting your back and going to the chiropractor, poison ivy, chipped teeth, break your wrist, sprain your ankle, burns, stitches, something falls in your eye…those are all 'getting hurt'. Now everything either falls under 1 of 2 categories, either get hurt or get sick. 'This' is the get sick version. The accident is still our most popular plan that I think everyone should have, but about half of the people ask about the sickness version, and that's this one."

This plan works 2 ways. First of all every time you go to the doctor for really 'anything', from a physical to an ear ache, to something major, you get $25/visit. That is kind of intended to cover a co-pay that someone may have. I don't even need a doctor's note for this one, it's on the honor system. Just let me know you went, and you get $25 within days. That's 4 times a year for an individual, 8 for a family, so on this one you are actually getting $200 back. But if you are *hospitalized* because of a 'sickness', that's what this one is really for. You get $1000 for being admitted (I quote it with the initial hospitalization rider, all units), plus $100 a day you're there, unless you are there for more than 2 weeks, then it doubles to $1400 a week, and that would last up to 6 months. There is also an ambulance benefit, MRI and CAT scan, rehab, again if it is because of a 'sickness'. And lastly a surgical benefit from $100 to $2000, $100 being something minor, the 2000 for an organ transplant. For example a vaginal childbirth is a $300 surgical benefit. So for childbirth for example, between the hospitalization and surgical benefit, you'd get about $1500 so Mom can stay home with the baby for a few weeks."

"When I sit with you for a minute 1 on 1, I can get you an exact price on that if you want once I have your date of birth in the computer..."

That 'second' policy should've been explained in about a minute; 2 minutes tops.

In situations where I only have literally fifteen to twenty minutes to enroll a half dozen drivers before they head out to the job site, I am happy with the 'accidents and out', and my record is presenting to and enrolling 9 hairstylists in under 45 minutes! I made a quick $600+, and they have since asked me back to see new hires, and for an explanation of the 'sickness' version, because I planted the seed before I left. However, that is all there was time for at this particular employee meeting, and the owner was both thankful and impressed that I was not insistent on monopolizing more time than that.

That being said, if I am awarded the opportunity to present for more like 10 to 12 minutes instead of 5 in front of the employees, and the employees are typically in the $15+/hour range, I think the 1-2 punch of accident and cancer is superb.

After my accident policy story-telling, I ask, "So far so good?" I then (like the sickness example above) remind them that the accident plan covers every situation from sprains, burns, chipped teeth, pulled backs, cuts, stitches etc, ... getting 'hurt'. I now shift into, "That is definitely our most popular policy, but this one right here is our second most popular policy, it is our cancer plan." I have a little fun at this point with a quick statistic and trivia question, "Now we do Aflac for dozens of the fire departments around here, and a quick stat I'll give you is this, 'the odds of your house burning down is 1 in 1500, but it could happen, that's why we have fire departments, and that's why you have to insure your mortgage. 1 in 1500. Now what do you think the chances are of say a man getting cancer? The closest guess gets to keep the free talking duck. What do you guess?'" I love it when the urge to guess in quest for the duck is irresistible, and someone belts out "1 in 100". I follow with, "Good guess, anybody else?" As different bids go around the room, I'll add a "It's free to guess" until almost everybody has had a chance. Then I say, "Who said 1 in 4?" The proud respondent speaks up. "Congratulations, you were the closest, but unfortunately, it's 1 in 2! ... for men, 1 in 3 for women." People are amazed when you produce that stat, and now you have their attention! Then I add, "If it runs in your family at all like it does mine, the odds are even higher."

I open the brochure and point to the stat, and say, "This is not a Jonny or an Aflac stat, this is according to the National Cancer Institute. If you get a chance, go to their website and you'll see not only the 1 in 2 stat highlighted, but the stat that cancer is a leading cause of bankruptcy in this country. And on the web site, almost every case study that they list had health insurance, but that's not what makes you lose your house. I do the claims, and just to give you an idea, say

God forbid, my wife came down with cancer, and the doctor says, "You've got to go to Boston" 3, 4 maybe 5 days a week for treatment, let me ask you, who do you think, out of everybody on this planet, she wants to drive her there? That's right…me! And I would, I'd be there holding her hand. But now you've got '2' people missing work 3, 4, or 5 days a week. And that can go on for months. Then at $4 a gallon, gas to Boston every day isn't free. And I went to a Red Sox game a few weeks ago, and let me tell you, parking in Boston is 'definitely' not free. Then you have co-pays, deductibles, hotels maybe, who's gonna watch the kids? And all the bills at home are still due, even though you both missed work. That's what rocks your world financially. That's where Aflac comes in!"

Depending on the group, I may or may not mention the initial diagnosis rider. If the employees are say $15/hour and up, I usually say, "First of all, God forbid you get that dreaded phone call, "I hate to say it, you've got the 'C' word" you are going to get a check for $2500 within about a week, just for being diagnosed. Unless it happens a year from now, then its $3000, the year after that $3500 etc, going up $500 a year until you need it. Then your kids are covered on the cancer plan for free, and their benefit is actually double. Say, God forbid, me or you get that call 3 years from now, 'Your kid's got cancer', you'd get a check within about a week for $8000. It's the same 1 page claim form as with the accident, it just says cancer at the top instead of accident. That's a sizeable sum of money, again so you can make some very important decisions, like, 'Where are we going to get our treatment?'"

"Then, the day you go for your first treatment, (radiation, chemo, oral, injection…) you get another check for $3000! Then you'll receive $900 a week as long as you need chemo (my mom had a little over a year of those altogether with her breast cancer, and then it came back on the other side.) My dad had prostate cancer and he didn't need the shots, but he had the radiation. This pays $500 a week for that. Also, that $500 or $900 a week isn't taxed, its also an indemnity plan, the same way the accident is. And there is no lifetime maximum. And we even pay you if you get experimental treatments, and health insurance doesn't even cover that!"

"And there are no lifetime maximums, you are not going to exhaust your benefits, this word right here 'n-o-n-e' (pointing to the word in the brochure). Hopefully you catch it early and your treatment plan is over in 3 months, and you're back on with your life, but we have some claims right now that are 10 and 11 years running, in and out of remission. I have a customer in Fitchburg, Mass that owns a small car dealership whose son wouldn't be alive today if he hadn't gotten a transplant. Stem cells or bone marrow, that's 'another' check for $10,000! And we give $1000 to the donor! It's a little easier to find a donor if you can give them 1000 bucks!"

"One other thing to keep in mind, is that even if you do have 'disability', most of the time you hopefully 'can' work. Disability always has that elimination period, so unless you are totally out of work for weeks at a time, it may not pay at all. Like my mom for example, she has more good days than bad, like "Yeah I'm gonna beat this thing", she may be real sick the day after a treatment, but most of the time she is doing good. We pay these benefits whether or not you're working."

"Then there's a surgical benefit, up to $6250 per."

"As cumulative as these all are so far, the 2 big ones are actually hospital and transportation. You are going to have days in the hospital if you are fighting cancer. There was an agent in our state that fought cancer for almost 10 years, unfortunately he did pass away right before Christmas 2 years ago, but his last 3 months, he was in a Boston, at Brigham and Women's Hospital. Because of this paragraph right here, his wife was able to take 3 months off and stay with him bedside right up to the very end, which is where she wanted to be. She could because of this benefit. On top of everything else, she was getting $18,000 a month. The last thing on her mind was, 'Is the mortgage going to get paid?' And 'he' had a lot of peace of mind knowing his family wasn't going homeless because he was sick. He was a 'huge' cheerleader for this, he had ducks all over his room."

"There's also a benefit for home health care, skilled nursing, God forbid hospice care. There's a benefit for reconstructive surgery, my mom had that with her breast cancer. Ambulance, not as likely as with the 'get hurt plan', but transportation… that's the other big one. We are pretty fortunate here in the northeast to have a lot of great hospitals. But even if you have to travel to Dartmouth 3, 4, 5 days a week, at $4 a gallon, that can really add up. We have a customer, a bank in North Conway, NH, where a young guy, a bank teller in his thirties… has to go to Baltimore, Maryland for his treatments! He has good health insurance with his bank that pays the hospital once he gets there, but this is what you use to drive or fly, should you have to go to Baltimore, or maybe the Mayo clinic in Minneapolis, UCLA, or Texas. By the way, kids are free to add to this plan, and if it's your child that has to travel, we pay a double benefit so that both parents can travel with their kid, and we pay toward hotels etc."

"Now thankfully we don't take blood samples, and there is no peeing in a cup. We just ask you 2 questions. 'Have you ever had cancer?' If it's a 'no', then you qualify. Even if it's a 'yes', but you've been treatment free or in remission for 5 years, you qualify."

"This one is done by date of birth, 'age-banded' we call it, but it runs probably some where between $5 to $14/week" (if I am quoting it with the IDR) or "somewhere between 4 and 11 dollars" (if I opted not to initially mention the IDR). It's a few dollars to add a spouse to this one, but kids are free, and can be covered on your plan now up to age 26."

Now the 'budget' close I think is crucial. I say, "Now believe it or not, we don't want to over-insure anybody. Some people have way too much insurance, they're insurance poor. Our job is to protect your paycheck, not blow it. Our mindset is that out of your entire work-week, (I spread out my hands about 3 feet apart), approximately 1 hour's worth of wages should protect your paycheck with Aflac. (I move my right hand in to within about 3 inches of my left). But for about the price of a pizza with toppings, you can probably get both family plans, and have a whole lot of peace of mind."

Another tool to at least get everybody 'to' the laptop, is saying, "If anyone wants prices on the cancer plan, I can sit with you for a second, enter your date of birth into the computer, and it will tell you 'exactly' how much it will run you, based on your age 'today', and then the price will never go up." Again, it's a great tool to at least get them to sit with me, which is why I never hand out rate sheets.

So many times, when I've offered the 1-2 punch, the mindset among the employees is not, "Should I get it?" but rather "Should I get both or just the 'blue' plan?"

If enrollment conditions are ideal, and I really 'have the floor' for an extended period of time, I might even offer 'The Big Three', or what our regional calls the 'catastrophic protection package', having critical care be the third. If I do actually present all 3 in front of the group, the pitch on the critical care/specified event plan is very brief. It's a 1 or 2 minute summary at best. My 'close' after presenting accident and cancer is, "Now again, we don't want to over-insure anybody, but for literally a few dollars a week, having the accident and cancer coverage gives you a lot of peace of mind. But some people may not have any cancer in their family history, but their father, brother, uncle, and grandfather have all had high blood pressure, heart issues or strokes. If that's the case then this third plan, called critical care may make more sense for you. It basically works 2 ways. First of all (quoting plan 2), any reason at all you find yourself in intensive care, you are going to get $700/day for the first week, $1200/day for the second week. Quick math, that's about $15,000 within two weeks in ICU. Then, if its something on this list of major events like heart attack, stroke, renal-failure, major organ transplant... you get an additional $5000. With most of those things, you'd have at least 2 weeks in ICU, so that's $20,000 within 2 weeks of having a major heart attack or stroke. Again, that's way more than disability could ever legally pay you. Then, if it is one of those major events, there's going to be a lot of follow up care. This pays another $9000/month for further hospitalizations, $125 any day you have a doctor visit, from dietary consults to speech therapy if you had a stroke. The ambulance, travel, hotels etc work very similar to the other two plans, but the other big one is another check for $25,000 if you needed a major organ transplant like a heart or lung. That can buy you a whole lot of time if you are on a waiting list. This plan is also 'age-banded', but it usually a little less than the cancer plan, maybe $3 to $10 a week. With this one there are just a couple health questions, but unless you are an insulin diabetic or have had a heart attack 'lately', you probably qualify."

This blitz of the critical care brochure should be a literal 2 minute overview tops.

Again, specific instructions are vital at the end of your presentation to get the enrollment process started. "Just a quick recap, the accident, which I think everyone should have is $5.05 a week." (or whatever the SIC rate is) "The other two are age banded, but average about the same. Again, we don't want to over-insure anybody, so consider about an hour's worth of wages to protect the rest of your paycheck with Aflac. If somebody wanted all 3, it might be about $16, and with pre-tax savings, around $11.50." (if that applies), "So literally for the price of a pizza with toppings, you could probably get all 3 plans. If your spouse can't get Aflac where he or she works, then an hour of your wage and an hour of theirs together is way more than enough for all 3 family plans. We will sit with you 1 on 1 to see what makes the most sense."

Now as you sit 1 on 1 with people, consider yourself a consultant. I typically get their basic information into the computer, and quickly fill out the accident app., and then ask, "Does cancer run in your family?" If they answer yes, they usually sell themselves on getting the coverage.

I almost didn't write this chapter, for fear of new agents abandoning the 'accidents and out' mindset, and writing a bunch of businesses quick. I still highly recommend you do several of those first, get a bunch of groups closed, get paid, and do any up-selling at the laptop. There is always a chance of losing the sale altogether if you complicate it, and to this day, I quite often just present the accident.

I recently wrote a group where a previous rep had gone in months before, bored them with a long explanation, and left them a folder full of 11 different brochures! It's no wonder they didn't proceed.

Keep it simple, make it quick, and just keep the 1-2 punch up your sleeve.

SERVICING: THE FOUR
MAGIC QUESTIONS

R emembering the reason we sell insurance, we want to make a
lot of money now, but also create a substantial residual income
for years to come.

This requires some service from you, not just the "Wham-bam-
thank-you-ma'am" at the initial enrollment.

For starters, there is nothing worse than being 'way' over volume
for a free trip, but finding out that your 'no-pay' rate exceeds 13%...
ask me how I know.

It is essential that you stay in contact with that account not only
up to the enrollment, but through that first deduction, and then when
their first invoice arrives.

I've got to tell you, this was my biggest weakness when I started.
I was so focused on signing four to eight groups a week, that I took
very little time to make sure that things went smooth for my accounts
come first invoice time.

I still have to make a conscious effort not to wane in this area, but
I am much better than I used to be.

I literally had the naïve mentality of, "I'll sign 'em up faster than they can quit", but that was stupid. I could have easily avoided substantial charge-backs, and my income would have grown even faster.

I recently heard the stat that most former Aflac groups that no longer do business with us, eventually parted ways for the #1 reason that their agent vanished from the face of the earth after the initial enrollment.

So, to solidify that relationship between you and your accounts, and to protect your long-term residual income, stay close to all of your account managers, and resolve every issue while they are insignificant, and win their confidence.

But even after that first invoice is paid on time, 'please' make it a point to give a courtesy call at least every 90 days. While you definitely don't want to wear out your welcome, you certainly want that account to know you care, are available, and can resolve any issues that may arise.

Even when things are running smooth, call every 90 days and ask the '4 magic questions'. Ideally, what's the best thing that could occur at an existing account...new hires eligible for Aflac, right? But to tactfully work our way back in there, try these four questions, with the 'new employee' question coming last.

"Hi Mrs. Jones, how's everything going? 'Just giving you a courtesy call to see if there are any questions or issues:

1. Are your invoices still coming on time, to the proper address, and seem accurate?

2. Are there any claims that you are aware of?

3. Has anyone left or been terminated?

4. Are there any new hires since we last spoke?

By asking the first question, he or she knows that if a billing question does arise, you'll be there to address it. Secondly, the claims question is to remind her that if there is a claim out there, "just have them call me", it's not her responsibility. Thirdly-employees which have gone: If we are diligent about this, we can contact that former employee and remind them that they can continue their Aflac coverage at the group rate, even though they are no longer with that company. It may very well be an opportunity to bring Aflac to their 'new' job as well. Finally, we want access to make money presenting to the new hires.

Just be sure to keep that HR lady very happy. A little stuffed talking duck can go a long way.

And be transparent. If you make a mistake, then admit to it, and rectify it, rather than excusing a mistake and shifting the blame.

It can actually be a blessing, and in a weird way an opportunity to solidify a relationship when there is a glitch, regardless of who's at fault. You can actually work together to rectify it.

FOR WHAT IT'S WORTH:
"YOU ARE NOT ALONE"

There are seasons where you've got the mojo happening. I mean serious momentum is building, and your fan-fare is behind you all the way.

But what about those moments when everything seemingly falls apart, and the cheerleaders you had on the mountaintop are nowhere to be found. It is in these moments when you are most alone. It's these times that mold you, or if you succumb to the circumstances and outside influences, actually break you. Hopefully your upper (district/regional) is there to encourage you. 'Maybe' you have the loving support of your spouse or family, maybe a best friend, or mentor. But maybe, perhaps 'probably', there are defining moments when you are in fact alone.

Catastrophic events level you financially. Absolute betrayal in a relationship devastates you emotionally. Injustice has its way with you. To some degree, we will all have to go through seasons like this. A crossroads if you will, that can determine your outcome, your timeline for success certainly, or even your destiny.

In these moments of soul searching and wondering "Why?!", you are alone.

But I am here to tell you that its in these defining moments, you are 'not' alone... This is where your faith is both forged and determined.

Faith, by definition, is the 'substance of things hoped for, and the evidence of things not yet seen'. These are the seasons of your life where you can learn to lean on something bigger than yourself, something larger than life itself, to accompany you, or at times even carry you, to the other side, across the desert, to victory, to safety...whatever.

Now this is a chapter on faith, but it is 'not' a chapter on religion. To me, religion can't help me. In my opinion religion is a bunch of oppressive rules made up by imperfect men, intended to oppress society, lord over people, and even make a profit off them. When my world falls apart, that's definitely not what I need.

No, I'm talking about going directly to the author of life itself. The Infinite Source of Intelligence. Tapping into a Higher-Power, most often referred to as 'God'.

Again, in those moments when you've done all you can, the walls are closing in, and you're all alone...I'm here to say, you're 'not' alone.

I'm going to share with you now some very personal 'valley' experiences I've had. Some defining moments where my own world was literally crashing down, and I was very 'alone'. During those times, my family 'tried' to help me. Religion couldn't help me, and I certainly didn't need any more 'rules' to help me, but I desperately needed to know that I wasn't alone.

It was the late 90's. I owned a martial arts studio in New Hampshire. I had 5 babies at home, ages 1 to 7. I had just bought a house, and from the surface, I appeared to be successful and have a storybook family. But as is often the case, things weren't quite as they seemed. Even though I did have control of my attitude, and I almost always remained positive and hopeful, circumstances that for the most part were way beyond my control began to turn my world upside down.

My wife at the time had always been challenging, and seemed to always live off of strife and chaos. Instead of refusing to let the events of her childhood determine who she would become, she instead seemed to embrace her childhood heartaches and dysfunction, and used them as an eternal green-light to be forever a victim of circumstance, an 'excuse' for inexcusable behavior if you will.

Her behavior started to become extreme after the birth of our fifth child. Not only were there several affairs, but she began to run with the wrong crowd and live the party life. She would even disappear, especially on a Friday night, unaccounted for. On many a Saturday morning, I would be stranded at home with five babies, while two miles down the road, mothers with their children were lined up outside my karate school, wondering where the teacher was. I couldn't just leave my children unattended, and as you can imagine, many of my students' parents did not tolerate the situation, and rightfully so. Furthermore, my ex had begun to ride an emotional roller coaster. When she was on a high, her behavior was out of control. Then when she crashed, she was suicidal, resulting in many overdoses and trips to the ER. She even needed surgical repair after one attempt, to reattach the tendons in both forearms, after cutting both of her wrists. In between several serious attempts, there were several 'attention-grab' overdoses, to get the light off of her behaviors. None-the-less, every time I got the '911' message on my pager,(many times while I was teaching a class) I would have to rush home to make sure she was alive, conscious, and safe. Needless to say, it was a very tough environment with which to operate a karate school.

Yet 'something' seemed to prompt me to start a delivery business for the Boston area, about an hour south of where I lived. A random ad for a company seeking a delivery service in an out-of-state paper somehow caught my eye. One thing led to another, and though it made no sense at all, I followed my gut instinct and started to develop a customer base which included British Airways at Logan Airport (delivering lost luggage) and a huge pharmacy in Peabody, Mass that often needed rush deliveries to nursing homes an hour or so in any direction.

None of this made sense. There were times when I would fight traffic for an hour just getting into Boston, just to have to turn around and respond to another '911' on my pager (usually a attention-grab false alarm). I was still trying to keep the karate school doors open and now I was doing overnight deliveries. I had to buy two delivery vans. It was another venture as self-employed, so there were of course no benefits of any kind etc. It made no sense, but my gut kept saying, "Trust me, do it."

I began to pray, a lot. I literally was begging God to tell me if I was crazy, or was this what I was supposed to be doing? But I wasn't getting an answer. There was no thundering voice from the sky, no signs in the heavens, just this prompting in my intuition.

Pretty early on in the venture, I got a page at 2:30 am. It was my first 'long-bomb'. (As a courier service you coveted these because they paid hundreds of dollars.) If I could get to RR Donnelly Printers in Hudson, Massachusetts, pick up some time sensitive materials, and deliver them to a company in Albany, New York by 7am, I would get paid hundreds of dollars for the job. "Yee haw!"

I picked up the printing, and headed west. I remember spending a couple of hours 'w/God' alone in the van on the way out there. Somehow I knew he was with me. I was still crying out to him for an answer to this whole idea, but I had a peace about me knowing that I wasn't alone.

It was about 6:30 when I realized I didn't really know where I was going. I just knew if you took the Mass Turnpike (route 90) west, it eventually turns into the New York Throughway, and eventually you will come to Albany. I didn't have a map or anything, I just figured I would get close, then figure it out or ask for help.

Time was running out, and then my heart sank when the throughway came into Albany. If you've ever been there, its an instant octopus maze of ramps going in every direction. My instant prayer was, "God, I need your help on this one!" Eenie, Meanie, Minie, Moe...I picked a ramp and started driving aimlessly toward tall buildings. I couldn't find a single open gas station or store that was open, and it was just barely getting light out, (and getting dangerously close to 7:00). Finally I saw a guy, walking quickly down the sidewalk in a suit with a briefcase in his hand. I pulled along side him, rolled down the passenger window, and asked, "Excuse me sir, have you ever heard of this address, this company, this street?..."

He said, "Yeah, you're in the loading dock!"

A rush of amazement came over me. I pounded on the door, and got a janitor to sign for the delivery at 2 minutes before 7. I called in the POD (proof of delivery) and I got paid for the job! Hallelujah, that was a miracle!

I was so excited on the way back, I could hardly stand it. I knew with every ounce of my being that that had been a 'God-thing'. The creator of the universe had just reached down to help 'me'. As I drove, what I can only refer to as the presence of God 'filled' my van. (My arms are chilled now as I am writing and recall this experience). The presence was so thick, like a cloud, that I felt you could have cut it with a knife. Not in my ears, but somehow in my soul, I heard, "You are exactly where I want you." I had my answer. I no longer thought I was crazy with this whole delivery business notion. Although it still seemed to make no sense, I somehow knew I was where I was supposed to be.

A few weeks later, my ex-wife was in a psychiatric hospital for almost five months straight, and I had to bring all five kids to work with me every single day. But by that time, I had acquired enough of a customer base to keep me busy.

Now hear this, it wasn't easy. In fact it was crazy. Driving overnight at times to New Jersey while they all slept in the van. I was changing diapers and mixing formula bottles in downtown Boston loading docks and freight elevators. Even home-schooling my son Dusty in the front seat! It was beyond crazy, but then we actually became almost like celebrities with various customers. Secretaries and nurses would be waiting for us with five candies lined up on their desk. Somehow God gave me strength to endure that season, but more than that, thinking back now- what other profession in the world would I have been able to do and bring five very small children to work every day?! I couldn't teach, work a warehouse, restaurant or construction. What else but a self-employed delivery driver? God, in his infinite wisdom and love, had already known what the next season of our lives was going to be like, and he had preplanned a way for me to support my kids.

Now that's not religion, but that is what I believe is Jesus Christ, alive and well, showing himself faithful and true.

There is a verse in the Good Book (Proverbs 3:5+6) that says, "Trust God with all your heart, and don't lean on your own understanding. In all your ways acknowledge Him, and he 'will' direct your paths".

I have so many 'God-stories' similar to this one that I would love to share with you. If you are going to put this fast-track system from this book to work for you, you'll be winning many trips, and whether on a Convention trip, cruise, or President's Club, I would love to share more of my 'God-encounters' with anyone who looks me up, over a coffee or a beer. But my experiences are not because I am anything special, but only because I believe and have faith. "The same God who takes care of me, shall also provide all of your needs..." (Philippians 4)

Dare to believe. Both the peace and the confidence that come from knowing 'you're not alone' is amazing. Knowing God is for you, with you, and behind you, 'Now' what do you dare to accomplish?

I'm not putting down anyone's religion. Religion isn't always a bad thing at all. It can offer a lot of self-discipline in your life, and it suggests a good moral standard and strong family values. But it's a 'relationship' with Him that can actually help you.

I know a lot of people have a lot of different ideas of who God is. However, I look at it this way. The calendar declares that something so entirely radical occurred about '2010' years ago... a guy walked out of the grave days after being publicly tortured and executed. Hundreds of eyewitnesses, even when it costs them their own life, declared, "I swear I saw the man, he's alive!" Now I really do believe that Confucius, Buddha, Mohammed among others were very good people. Amazing in their views of trying to change the world and make it a better place. But, they all died, they are still dead, and you can even visit their graves. But the tomb in Jerusalem is still empty!

Whatever your perception of who God is to you, I encourage you to cling to Him, lean on Him, and believe. With Him, you can accomplish whatever you can dream. Just remember, you are never alone.

One more story, just to rule out the ridiculous notion that it is always 'coincidence':

Fast forwarding from the last story, I had by this point already been awarded full custody of my five children, and was a single dad. Although I was doing my best, I had had to spend most of my money on legal fees to ensure that I was awarded full custody of my son and four daughters. I couldn't afford to stay where I was, so I was forced to find an apartment. But who in their right mind would rent to a guy with five kids, plus a dog, not to mention... didn't have any money. But I had to start looking.

My oldest daughter actually found a house to rent, in the north end (nice part) of Manchester. We all went to see it on that Saturday night. All the kids agreed, "This is it dad, we love it…that's my room…" The landlord wasn't crazy about the dog thing, but was impressed with the behavior of the children, and after a firm handshake, he looked in my eyes and said, "You know what Jonny, I want you to have the place. If you want it, bring me the $1750 security deposit by Wednesday and it's yours."

'Yee haw' right? Only problem… I didn't have any money.

That was Saturday night. The next morning, I took all of the kids to church, and I spent some time at the alter with God and said, "All right God, if this is the place you have in mind for me and the kids, you've got to come up with $1750 in the next couple of days, cuz I've got nothing. So, 'It's all on you God'".

There was literally nothing else I could do at that point, so I left it in His hands.

Monday night, after teaching an MMA class, one of my students, Jonathan, mentioned that I had left some stuff at his house. So I stopped by there on the way home. One thing I had left there was a pair of jeans, and there was $150 in the front pocket. Nice!

While I was teaching, my oldest daughter had listed my king-size bedroom set on Craig's List (since it wouldn't fit in the new place). She got a response, "I live in Florida, but I also own a company in New Hampshire. I am looking to furnish my lake house up in Weare. I will offer you $1600, site unseen. And, I'll have one of my crews come by tomorrow with a box truck to pay you in cash, and pick up the set."

Unbelievable! They did indeed show up on Tuesday night, didn't even ask for help carrying it all out, and handed me $1600. Add that to the $150 from the pair of jeans. I handed the landlord $1750 on Wednesday and said, "I'll take it."

Now that's not religion, and it's not some intangible vague mystical life-force to feel good about. In my opinion, that was JC, alive and well, coming through for me 'again', in a really big way.

I dare you to really get to know Him, dare to let Him help you. He will never let you down. "Whoever calls upon the name of the Lord will never be disappointed!" (Romans 10:11)

PARTING WORDS OF WISDOM

I wish you much success as you build your Aflac business. Please stay true to the course. Keep your goals in front of you, don't drift from the game plan, and never, never give up. Dare to dream bigger every month. Constantly keep score.

One asset that has really driven our district is the book *Success Principles*, by Jack Canfield. Of all the books I've read on success, positive thinking, and sales skills, I believe this is the best. If you've ever read the classic *Think and Grow Rich*, this is a modern day, updated version of that. I literally expect every member of my team to read a chapter-a-day. Any agent who wants my help in the field must demonstrate 3 regimented practices.

1. Book 10 appointments 'every' week

2. Read a chapter in *Success Principals* each day

3. And take time each day reviewing, clarifying, and visualizing their goals

I truly believe that success is certain if your activity is honest, and you keep your clearly defined purpose in front of you. Maintain your integrity, always. Look out for other people. Stay close to others on a similar journey. It's tougher to do it alone. Stay accountable to a mentor.

My agents are asked the same questions almost every Friday, "Did you book 10?" and "Are you still reading a chapter a day?"

Staying accountable means that if you have only booked 8 appointments this week, and its 4:00 on a Friday afternoon, you don't go home yet, even if you've closed 4 groups this week.

Be on time, and keep your word. That's everything.

There are a lot of fantastic people in this company who have a whole lot to offer, and have been around for way longer than I have, and have been tremendously successful. Take any help you can get, stay completely teachable, and commit to never-ending improvement. Before long it will be your turn to pass the vision on to others.

I hope I have been able to help you or inspire you in some way. Thank you so much for allowing me to share myself with you.

Much success! I'll see you at the top!

God be with you, -Jonny

About the Author

Jonny Burgess is newer to Aflac than most coordinators, being just 2 and a half years in the business.

Prior to Aflac, Jonny was a single father with 5 kids at home, engaged to be married, and his 10-year gourmet food sales business had just gone under due to the economy. He also owns Team Burgess' Studios, training mixed martial arts cage-fighters.

Having had to recover from a bad car accident in 1999 that almost left him crippled, and subsequently losing his home, Jonny was starting over once again 10 years later.

Regional Bill Henry, a friend of his fiancé, presented the Aflac opportunity to Jonny, and he got licensed at the end of 2008, thinking a second line of income could supplement his struggling food business.

In January 2009, he was forced to close his food business completely, and found himself full-time with Aflac.

With just weeks until his wedding, Jonny 'had' to make a lot of money fast, so he created a plan, invented a 'system', and went to work.

He opened and enrolled 21 groups in his first 7 weeks full-time with Aflac!

Jonny went on to become the #1 account opener in the country in his rookie year, opening over 72 accounts in 11 months.

Less than a year in the business, he was promoted to DSC, and began teaching others his 'system'.

After 1 year as a DSC, he was recognized on the FAME trip in Arizona as the runner-up 'Best-of-the-Best', ranking the #2 DSC in the country.

His fast-track system has become so effective, it has in part been adopted in his state's Sales School curriculum, and Jonny has been asked to speak to many other states as well.

Today Jonny lives in Bedford, NH with his wife Michelle, with six of their eight children still at home.

One thing I did throughout my first year, was monitor my own activity:

BECAUSE NUMBERS DON'T LIE!

So I have included a sample 'activity' chart like I used to use. I would simply hash mark any activity that qualified for that particular column. At first, I made sure in the 'BOOK – 2' column, I had at least 2 hash marks by the end of the day. Two hashes each day meant that at the end of the week, my total was at least ten. When I became ambitiously lazy, it revolutionized into 10 hashes on Monday, and then I was done for the week. If there was perhaps a contest going on, there were weeks when I booked 20 plus, but 10 was the absolute-minimum-Mendoza-can't go home yet threshold.

Please feel free to use the chart for yourself. You may find a different method to keep track, and that's fine, but I encourage you to make sure you 'don't' wait until the end of the day to fill it out. Fill it out on the fly. Make it a game. If you feel like you 'worked' today, check your activity chart to make sure you are doing enough of the right things, not busy-work, but the things that actually make you money.

Have fun with it, and keep yourself accountable.

Want to give yourself a raise? Go ahead. Make 'Book 15' and 'RUN 15' be the new threshold, and you will make more money!

Activity Chart	BOOK 2	RUN 2	M-1's	GROUPS	POLICIES
Monday					
Tuesday					
Wednesday					
Thursday					
Friday					
(Saturday)					
Weekly Totals:					

Activity Chart	BOOK 2	RUN 2	M-1's	GROUPS	POLICIES
Monday					
Tuesday					
Wednesday					
Thursday					
Friday					
(Saturday)					
Weekly Totals:					

Activity Chart	BOOK 2	RUN 2	M-1's	GROUPS	POLICIES
Monday					
Tuesday					
Wednesday					
Thursday					
Friday					
(Saturday)					
Weekly Totals:					

Activity Chart	BOOK 2	RUN 2	M-1's	GROUPS	POLICIES
Monday					
Tuesday					
Wednesday					
Thursday					
Friday					
(Saturday)					
Weekly Totals:					

Activity Chart	BOOK 2	RUN 2	M-1's	GROUPS	POLICIES
Monday					
Tuesday					
Wednesday					
Thursday					
Friday					
(Saturday)					
Weekly Totals:					

Activity Chart	BOOK 2	RUN 2	M-1's	GROUPS	POLICIES
Monday					
Tuesday					
Wednesday					
Thursday					
Friday					
(Saturday)					
Weekly Totals:					

Activity Chart	BOOK 2	RUN 2	M-1's	GROUPS	POLICIES
Monday					
Tuesday					
Wednesday					
Thursday					
Friday					
(Saturday)					
Weekly Totals:					

Activity Chart	BOOK 2	RUN 2	M-1's	GROUPS	POLICIES
Monday					
Tuesday					
Wednesday					
Thursday					
Friday					
(Saturday)					
Weekly Totals:					

Activity Chart	BOOK 2	RUN 2	M-1's	GROUPS	POLICIES
Monday					
Tuesday					
Wednesday					
Thursday					
Friday					
(Saturday)					
Weekly Totals:					

Activity Chart	BOOK 2	RUN 2	M-1's	GROUPS	POLICIES
Monday					
Tuesday					
Wednesday					
Thursday					
Friday					
(Saturday)					
Weekly Totals:					

Activity Chart	BOOK 2	RUN 2	M-1's	GROUPS	POLICIES
Monday					
Tuesday					
Wednesday					
Thursday					
Friday					
(Saturday)					
Weekly Totals:					

CPSIA information can be obtained
at www.ICGtesting.com
Printed in the USA
LVOW11s2327150517
534653LV00001B/100/P